HOW TO
TURN
YOUR
CHILD
INTO A
DOORMAT

ISBN 978-1-64468-972-1 (Paperback)
ISBN 978-1-64468-973-8 (Digital)

This publication contains the opinions and ideas of the author. It is intended to provide helpful and informative material on the subjects addressed in the publication. It is sold with the understanding that the author and publisher are not engaged in rendering medical, health, psychological, or any other kind of personal professional services in the book. If the reader requires personal, medical, health, or other assistance or advice, a competent professional should be consulted.

The author and publisher specifically disclaim all responsibility for any liability, loss or risk, personal or otherwise, that is incurred as a consequence, directly or indirectly, of the use and application of the contents of this book.

Covenant Books, Inc.
11661 Hwy 707
Murrells Inlet, SC 29576
www.covenantbooks.com

HOW TO
TURN
YOUR
CHILD
INTO A
DOORMAT

A PERSONAL ACCOUNT OF GROWING UP IN THE SHADOW OF A NARCISSIST

SYDNEY KISAI

*To my therapist, who so embodies our Lord
that she drew me out of the shadows…to become a therapist myself,
my pastor and spiritual father, who taught me to listen to the Invisible One,
whose hand has orchestrated this journey of healing.*

*Oh, praise the One who paid my debt
and raised this life up from the dead.*

—FROM THE HYMN, "JESUS PAID IT ALL"
BY ELVINA HALL

CONTENTS

FOREWORD

Three or four years ago, I furiously searched and dug, trying to find and assemble the pieces of my shattered self. About two o'clock in the morning I suddenly awoke and felt compelled to write. Something in my gut stirred to have a voice. My child self spoke nonstop for two whole pages. This is what she said:

> When my father wanted me to conform, it was as if he put me in the machines that crush cans and flatten them. I tried to make myself smaller so I wouldn't get as hurt, in an attempt to survive longer. Hammering, using sheer force, I felt myself utterly flattened like a can. When I dared to be myself, I became the adversary, the target; no room for me. He removed his love, leaving me alone. I felt abandoned, like I was walking a tightrope. I was an orphan... lost in the big world. Did anyone care about my pain? Did anyone think this was wrong? Trapped, I couldn't get away. When I broke, I felt humiliated. He loved me again, but I resented it. I yearned for love. Why did love equate with pain? If I wanted love, I had to cease to exist, disappear. I hated it when he rejected me, so I would do what he wanted. After a while, I figured him out, but I still cracked. I tried to convince myself that being withdrawn was better than caving in and doing what he wanted. He was too smart and strong, and I his lab rat, a pawn in his experiment to do with what

he wanted. He baited me with love, then conditioned me with rejection. Where did my voice go? Where did my rage go? Didn't anyone hear my cries? Did anyone see what was done to me? Could I have made this up? No, because I bear too many emotional scars. I am too messed up. I still feel the force and pressure of his will on me. I don't like it!

If he was beating me up, maybe I could have run away—but instead it was like he would drill himself into my brain like a worm in an apple. He would violate my mind and penetrate my head. I couldn't get away and he wouldn't stop. His pursuit of me had one goal: for me to be defeated and humiliated beyond recognition. I had to be assimilated, made indistinguishable, broken beyond repair. It is one thing to be defeated thousands of times. It is something else when your defeat is celebrated, almost as if your last shreds of dignity are cruelly taken, and you are left naked in your shame. He loved being better than me in everything, as if defeating and humiliating me was a food he craved. He relished every defeat, every humiliation and seemed to take special pleasure and joy out of crushing me. Like someone who enjoyed hurting animals who could not fend for themselves. Yet his abuse left no marks on my body—no trail that I could find later. Only brain fog. Like a cloud of confusion making me vulnerable to people like him. How in the world did I survive all these assaults? It must have been God. How do prisoners survive endless torture? No wonder I dreamed of escape. Who would believe me if I could even describe what was done to me with such methodical precision?

After rereading what I had just written, I felt struck by the clarity of the chosen words my small self used to describe and paint such a graphic picture of what happened. Seemed I was suddenly and abruptly transported to the scene of the crime. I could no longer deny that something terrible had happened to me. There was now a massive amount of evidence for what I would eventually come to identify as brainwashing. As I slowly came to accept what had happened to me as reality, my little self spoke up even more.

What do you say when there are no visible bruises of abuse but you sense someone's hands at your throat forcing you to swallow the sobs, dying to be released. Years pass and you're not able to feel when you want to, nor can you scream to free your voice. What do you do when you're raised by two 2 year olds who impose their realities on you, never allowing you the space to be yourself. Nonetheless, you love and adore them, leading you to believe this is normal and love always hurts. That is until you realize what you've lived through and survived was never normal. You're suddenly aware of your emotional stuntedness—you're sadly not like everyone else. You're missing pieces: you're different, but you can't figure out what's lacking.

Later, after much excavation into your past, you discover you had surgically removed those parts of yourself that caused you pain. Pieces of yourself like your ability to feel your feelings which became a liability to survival. You had to survive, but you're here with the missing pieces covered in ancient dirt. How can you scream now, more than fifty years later? How can you cry the sobs that stayed stuck in your throat seemingly forever? They are like mosquitos trapped in amber, in suspended animation, frozen in time. Then there's the confusion—it's been there all your life. Your reality intruded upon nearly erased by parents who were supposed to care and protect you, but were incapable of thinking beyond themselves.

No, it's all in your head. You can't trust your feelings. I told you I'd come back for you—why are you crying? It's not fair when you're a child, and an adult with their own agenda has the power and intellect to impose their will on you: so helpless, taking from you what was lacking in their own lives. Oblivious to the abuse, intent on survival, the world becomes a cruel, fearful place where needs are rarely, if ever, met and screams are never heard.

PREFACE

My intention in writing this book was not to create a handbook for turning a child into a doormat, but rather to provide an aid for adult children of narcissists to better understand what they have survived in order to move toward healing. Understanding is key due to the convoluted nature of narcissistic abuse. I consider myself something of a forensic therapist/archeologist, always on the hunt for discarded parts of myself, working to figure out what happened to me, and learning to integrate the recovered pieces. I have also discussed my history with my therapist, trying to make sense of my parents' bewildering behavior.

ACKNOWLEDGEMENTS

To those who encouraged me to write, and without whom this book would not exist, and to those who labored to make it a pleasure to read as it was to write.

INTRODUCTION

THIS IS NOT AN INSTRUCTION BOOK FOR ABUSING YOUR CHILD

During my nearly thirty-year journey to understand what happened to me (and why I was so messed up), I came across some interesting clues. Realizing my father was a narcissist was a huge piece of the puzzle, but discovering that narcissistic abuse appeared to include brainwashing techniques opened everything up for me. Delving deeper, I found commonalities in the experiences of POWs, domestic violence victims, and children of narcissists, as they all had experienced some form of brainwashing.

What follows are symptoms of narcissism in layman's terminology, as I find it easier for clarity's sake to speak in plain English vs. clinical terminology. These symptoms are drawn from Adult Children of Narcissistic Parent Resources. It is important to note that narcissism runs on a continuum with the more severe cases involving a form of sadism and sociopathology.

- a grandiose sense of self-importance (may be shown as an exaggeration of abilities and talents, expectation that she/he will be seen as superior to all others)

- is obsessed with him- or herself

- goals are almost always selfish and self-motivated

- has troubles with healthy, normal relationships

- becomes furious if criticized

- has fantasies of unbound success, power, intelligence, love, and beauty

- believes that he or she is unique and special, and therefore should only hang out with other special, high-status people

- requires extreme admiration for everything

- feels entitled—has unreasonable expectations of special treatment

- takes advantage of others to further his or her own needs

- has zero empathy—cannot (or will not) recognize the feelings of others

- may be envious of others or believe that others are envious of him or her

- behaves arrogantly, haughtily[1]

One of the inherent problems in discussing parental narcissistic abuse is that it is hard to believe a parent would treat their own child with such contempt and near lack of concern. The narcissistic parent manages to avoid detection by abusing under the radar; perpetuating severe emotional and mental abuse without those in the family system or outside world suspecting anything is wrong.[2] Hence, if it is difficult for anyone on the outside to pick up on the abuse, how much more challenging for the child in the middle of the confusion, to identify what is so seriously wrong with her chaotic world? Not only is it nearly impossible to articulate, most children would be resistant to believe that their parents are more interested in using rather than nurturing them. Still, most adult children of narcissists cannot deny the psychological damage they deal with on a daily basis. The average person would not expect a

1. "What Is Narcissistic Personality Disorder? What Are the Symptoms of Narcissistic Personality Disorder?" accessed November 11, 2015, www.bandbacktogether.com/adult-children-of-Narcissistic-parents-resources/, pages 1–2.
2. Krill Jr., William E., "The Child Victim of a Narcissistic Personality Disordered Parent," accessed October 25, 2017, https://wehavekids.com/family-relationships/the-child-victim-of-a-narcissistic-personality- Disordered-parent, page 1.

tortured prisoner of war to behave normally once released and returned to society. In many ways, children of narcissists are also survivors of brainwashing, and thus need time to deprogram and find themselves in order to heal.

It bears mentioning here that narcissistic abuse (inclusive of brainwashing) is not limited to the abuse of children, domestic violence victims, and POWs, but may also be present in nearly any type of relationship, including those in the workplace environment, friendships, and business partnerships, to name a few.

"Anyone willing to use known principles of control and reactions to control and capable of demonstrating the patience needed in raising a child can probably achieve successful brainwashing."[3]

We now know that men can be made to do exactly anything.… It's all a question of finding the right means. If only we take enough trouble and go sufficiently slowly, we can make him kill his aged parents and eat them in a stew.

(Romains, Jules. Verdun. 156. A. A, Knopf, 1939)[4]

3. Central Intelligence Agency, "Brainwashing from a Psychological Viewpoint," accessed November 21, 2018, www.cia.gov/library/readingroom/docs/CIA-RDP65-00756R000400050004-9.pdf 38.
4. Declassified Documents 1984, Microfilms under MKULTRA (84) 002258, Central Intelligence Agency, Washington 25, DC, Office of the Director, April 1956, Research Publication (Woodbridge, CT: 1956), page 3.

CHAPTER 1

BRAINWASHING IS THE COMMON DENOMINATOR IN MANY FORMS OF ABUSE

The Central Intelligence Agency published a report on Communist Brainwashing in April 1956. Under the section, Principles of Human Control and Reaction to Control, they listed steps to exercising control over an individual and changing his behavior and personal integration, as quoted below:

- Make the individual aware of control is the first stage in changing his behavior. The individual realizes that definite limits have been put upon the ways he can respond.

- The individual realizes that his survival is dependent on the controlling system. The controlled adult is forced to accept the fact that food, tobacco, praise, and the only social contact that he will get come from the very interrogator who exercises control over him.

- The awareness of control and recognition of dependence result in causing internal conflict and breakdown of previous patterns of behavior. Since the brainwasher-interrogator's aim is to have the individuals undergo profound emotional change, they force their victims to seek out painfully what is desired by the controlling individual.

- Discovery that there is an acceptable solution to his problem is the first stage in reducing the individual's conflict. Compliance brings relief to the internal conflict but causes him to lose his ability to be critical.

- Reintegration of values and identification with the controlling system is the final stage in changing the behavior of the controlled individual. [5]

So how do narcissistic parents abuse their children? The following is a list of control mechanisms that narcissist parents employ, as derived from Adult Children of Narcissistic Parent Resources. Note the similarities to the brainwashing steps listed above.

- puts parental needs far above those of the children
- promotes and fosters a dependent relationship between parent and child
- neglects needs of the child
- makes child feel as though he/she does not matter
- treats others as objects not people
- ignores personal boundaries
- distorts the concept of "love"
- manipulation for pleasure
- subtly and not subtly insults children
- ignores and overwhelms the children
- says one thing one day, something else the next
- untrustworthy
- compulsively lying to children
- uses the child's vulnerabilities to exploit the child
- makes child feel as though he or she is insane
- mold children to an "ideal" image[6]

---

5. *Declassified*, pages 2–3.
6. *Narcissistic Personality*, pages 5–6.

CHAPTER 2

ISOLATION

According to the CIA, the regimen within the detention cell is in itself a most formidable weapon in the arsenal of the captor, effectively breaking the will of prisoners. Prison officers are so confident in its effectiveness, they boast that there is literally no man who cannot be brought to do their bidding. Estimations are that it takes from four to six weeks of rigid, total isolation to "reduce prisoners to animals." The effects of isolation, anxiety, fatigue, sleep deprivation, uncomfortable temperatures, and chronic hunger produce disturbances of mood, attitudes, and behavior in nearly all prisoners. In other words, the prisoner's ability to resist the efforts and agenda of his captor are severely compromised as he is crippled in his ability to manage his emotions and think clearly enough in order to defend himself.[7]

The child of a narcissist endures isolation, but obviously not to the extent of a prisoner of war. Her prison is invisible. She can't escape because she is a child who is dependent on her parents to survive. While young, her parents are possessively close because she is a source of self-esteem (supplying the attention they require by adoring, admiring, and fearing them, also known as narcissistic supply). When she grows to become more independent, she may elicit envy from her parents who utilize manipulative and malevolent techniques to infantacize the child, keeping her dependent on them. To a young child... her parents are like powerful giants with a near lack of concern for her. She is completely

---

7. *Brainwashing*, pages 18–25.

at their mercy and disposal. The only real interest they have is in the child providing them with narcissistic supply (stroking their egos) and narcissistic feeding (treating the child with cruelty and contempt for the express purpose of feeding on her suffering by exerting their superiority and strength). In this sense, she is comparable to prisoners of war who are systematically abused. Like prisoners, attempts at asserting her feelings, rights, or thoughts (or simply trying to grow up) lead to even bigger problems; so she resorts to stifling her feelings to keep the peace. She lives with the constant tension of never knowing what is going to set her parents into a narcissistic rage, similar to a prisoner never knowing what is going to set off the guards.

My family did not resemble normal in any sense of the word. We were more like isolated islands or individuals living their own independent lives, who occasionally bumped into each other.

It was a lonely existence. At some point, I decided I had enough of my family, and the time to run away and escape had come. My father mocked me and asked, "How are you going to survive out there? You have no money." Although he dampened my spirit by saying this, I found I could nevertheless still run away in my mind. My books became my close friends, in large part because my interpersonal skills were so poor. Books like *From the Mixed-Up Files of Mrs. Basil E. Frankweiler* (the lead character left home to live in a museum) and *Pippi Longstocking* (she was a very independent child who pretty much lived on her own and did her own thing) encouraged and inspired me. *The Little House on the Prairie* television series also served to paint a picture of family normalcy for me. While growing up, I discovered my small self was a fighter and did not like to give up. Instead of recognizing this as a strength of mine, my parents minimized it and labelled it as "stubbornness." I, in no way, deny I have a streak of stubbornness, but I came to perceive it with a negative spin, as my parents did. That is, until I told my therapist some stories that exemplified this part of me, and she was delighted and laughing at my antics. I felt vindicated.

As an adult, when I began working as a Marriage and Family Therapist intern, I worked at over ten different clinics. Unfortunately, the people in management tended to be emotionally abusive, and I would end up quitting. Admittedly, I got a kind of thrill at having the power to quit. I asked my colleagues about how things were at other clinics, and they informed me they were also mistreated by management. Nevertheless, I felt ashamed about this track record/pattern and wanted my impulsive behavior to stop. I discovered through therapy my quitting was because of the option to escape the abusive management—something I didn't have as a child. Once I discovered the connection to my past, I was finally able to stop the behavior.

A prisoner in isolation is not allowed to communicate with anyone except his captor, and then only during interrogation sessions. Controlling communication is one of the most effective methods of producing a sense of helplessness and despair; as human beings are social creatures. It may well be the cornerstone of the Communist system of control. The prisoner comes to develop extreme dependency on the interrogator, as his only opportunity for the socialization for which he craves, ironically is with the very one in charge of his brainwashing and abuse. As a result, he loses yet another prop for his morale.[8] Similarly, a child of a narcissist is explicitly forbidden to discuss the communication (meaning to comment about the actions and communication of others); metacommunication, all of which are essential for developing successful social discourse. To be able to say such things as, "I feel uncomfortable when you look at me that way," "Are you serious?" or "What exactly did you mean by that?" In order for us to accurately decipher the meaning of our own or another's communication, we must be able to comment on what was said. The child of a narcissist is effectively restricted from such commentary.

When this issue came up in therapy, I continued to operate under the ancient premise that I wasn't allowed to metacommunicate about

8. *Declassified*, pages 4–5.

the things we talked about. This unspoken rule had been ingrained in me since childhood, yet I was completely oblivious to it. My therapist corrected me, and a whole new world opened up. More about this in Chapter 7.

When it came to my relationship with my ex-husband, isolation came first in the form of exclusivity. I mistook it for love. He "love bombed me" with flattery and attention. For my part, my low self-esteem had me believing that he was the best I could do. I believed that it was highly unlikely anyone else would show an interest in me. Then things began to shift in a negative direction as he gradually exerted more control. He told me he didn't like any of my friends and pressured me to live with him (where he would be better able to control me). Once I moved, he went through all of my things one by one, declaring to me that everything I owned was now his. When I inquired as to whether the reciprocal was also true, he gave me a pat answer of "of course," but I already knew he was lying.

What I realize now in hindsight is that I was so accustomed to being threatened and controlled from my past that it was no surprise that I chose to be with him. There were red flags everywhere, but I paid no heed. What I didn't realize until recently, however, was the extent of his narcissism. After he had gotten rid of all my friends (I didn't have very many), he decided to have a birthday party for me. It was the most awkward gathering I have ever attended in my whole life. It was held at his friend's home, and all of his friends were there. I finally realized he wasn't having a birthday party for me. He was instead having a gathering of friends for himself.

CHAPTER 3

EROSION OF THE SELF—
SURVIVAL AT ALL COSTS

In brainwashing, the end game is to scoop out the self of the prisoner and replace it with a compliant self (or a false self), a remade version conceived in the mind of the captor. For children of narcissists, the process of brainwashing begins even prior to the development of any semblance of a self. Freud once said that "the job of an infant is to survive." This couldn't be more true for the child of a narcissist. I learned early in life that my only hope of getting any of my needs met was by meeting my parents' needs first. I was conditioned to read their moods and cater to their needs, and this was what got reinforced. This later had a profound effect on my career choices. I also learned to put my needs last since their needs came first; mine were considered a bother and an imposition on them (placing your needs last is one of the distinct characteristics of someone who is codependent; i.e., addicted to a relationship). Any part of you that gets in the way of this singularized focus must be abandoned and metaphorically tossed off the ship as it becomes a major threat to your survival.

Alice Miller, author of *Drama of the Gifted Child: The Search for the True Self,* put it this way: "The reliability, continuity, and constancy that are so important for the child are therefore missing from this exploitative relationship. What is missing above all is the framework within which the child could experience his feelings and emotions. Instead, he develops something the mother needs and although this certainly saves his life (by securing the mother's or father's love) at the time, it may nevertheless prevent him, throughout his life, from being himself.[9]"

Looking back even further, a kind of "learned disappointment" is introduced to the infant, so any hope of connection and reciprocity has already begun to wither away. "Synchrony" is a process where parents reflect the infant's expressions to build rapport. The child experiences the joy of discovering that they can have an impact on the world around them. Instead, the child of a narcissist comes to realize that the focus isn't on her/him, but on the self-absorbed parents. What ends up happening is that the child will likely withdraw and give up hope of ever being recognized for who they are. Unfortunately, for the child of a narcissist, her/his emotional and psychological development will nearly always be overshadowed and truncated by the narcissistic parents. The world then becomes a scary, threatening, and sad place where emotional needs are rarely, if ever, met; and the child is systematically disappointed.

One of the hardest things I have had to grapple with was this truth—my parents never really loved me because they never knew me. In reality, I was just an extension of them, a means to an end, because everything was about them. For the longest time, I lived in denial of this, holding on to the belief that my childhood had been idyllic. As I learned more about what had really taken place, the layers of denial were gradually peeled away, and I could no longer deny what I knew to be true. It's a frightening thing when parents who are supposed to love and protect you choose instead to use and manipulate you. You are then very much alone in the world, and are trapped with no means of escape. I suppose this would explain what my paternal aunt told me as an adult, "You seemed depressed by the time you were two years old."

9. Miller, Alice, *The Drama of the Gifted Child: The Search for the True Self* (NY: Basic Books, 1997), 30.

CHAPTER 4

A METHOD TO THE MADNESS

Authorities will often observe their prisoners in order to customize and tailor their methods to best break down each individual prisoner.[10] For me "the carrot and the stick" was love. I was starving for it, so that became the bait they used to manipulate and coerce me into doing what they wanted. When I refused to comply, love would be quickly removed. Rejection, abandonment, or the silent treatment would quickly take its place until I broke. I always broke. What I noticed about the process was that my father enjoyed breaking me down. I hated myself for breaking down. I wished I was stronger. During those times when I managed to muster up enough courage to put up a fight, he would laugh and mock me, then take genuine pleasure in crushing me until I writhed, squirmed and cried.

I remember watching a prison movie a few years ago. It was called *The Experiment*[11] and was based on the Stanford Prison Experiment (held in 1973 by Zimbardo and his colleagues to determine whether the brutality of prison guards in America had more to do with the prison environment vs. the guards' personality type). [12] At the time, I had not yet realized that my father was a narcissist, nor was I aware of his abusive history with me. Thus, my reaction to the movie was puzzling and

10. *Declassified,* page 7.
11. *The Experiment*, Directed by Paul T. Scheuring. Performances by Adrien Brody, and Forest Whitaker. Inferno; Magnet; Mercator; Adelstein Productions, 2010.
12. McLeod, Saul, "The Stanford Prison Experiment," accessed December 19, 2018, https://simplypsychology.org/zimbardo.html, page 1.

concerning as I was at a loss to understand why I was so mesmerized by the conflictual relationship between a prison guard (Forest Whitaker) and a prisoner (Adrien Brody). The guard honed in on this one prisoner because of his disrespectful and defiant attitude. I didn't want him to break, and I rooted for him.

For prisoners, and for myself, defiance is like the last vestige of dignity you have left, and my father took great pleasure in taking it from me. For narcissists, feeding off the pain of their victims is literally like food to them. They love the kill. It makes them feel superior, and if you're a trapped lab rat like I was, they get to do it to you over and over again until you wish you never had a nervous system that enabled you to feel so much pain. It was like being hit with a cattle prod that fried your emotions to a crisp. My innocent self kept asking, "Why does love have to hurt?

CHAPTER 5

UNEXPECTED KINDNESS:
A DELIBERATE BREAKING DOWN OF DEFENSES

Unexpected kindness is the element of surprise. Friendliness on the part of the captor when least expected rattles the prisoner's ability to maintain a critical attitude.[13] It destabilizes the confidence he has in his ability to trust his perceptions and thereby protect himself in such a hostile, life-threatening environment. I wish to expound on this tactic a bit because of all the methods at the incarcerator's disposal, this happens to be his most successful. He chooses to use it precisely when the prisoner is near breakdown (due to the many imposed pressures and torture). When the prisoner returns once again to an interrogation session, expecting more torture and vilification, he finds a drastic change. The captor has completely transformed his demeanor and now offers him something to drink. Prisoners find this sudden kindness and release of pressure irresistible. Many end up producing confessions out of guilt and offering them as a kind of gift in response to the captor's kindness. I found this so true in my own case. My father could be incredibly cruel when he didn't get his way with me. After he vanquished me, he could be so sweet. At this point, I felt compelled, literally, to confess anything and everything I had done wrong, just like the tortured prisoner. I was never able to refrain myself because when he was kind to me, I automatically opened up, holding nothing back (despite my best efforts). The switching between cruelty and kindness inevitably wore me down.

---

13. *Brainwashing,* pages 37–39.

I remember, as a child, desperately wishing and hoping that my father would remain in his "kind mode" but inevitably, his dark side would show up. His behavior effectively kept me off balance and on constant edge because like a prisoner, I never knew which side of him would show up. In the article, "Brainwashing," the author summed up the conditioning process accordingly: "When you are in total darkness, a small light will grab your attention. When you are drowning in deep dread, you will grasp at any small straw of hope. When you are hurt, you will seek and be grateful for any rescue."[14]

Here are three other issues worth mentioning. First, this pattern of intermittent reinforcement (switching between kindness and cruelty) is highly addictive.[15] It reinforces the desired behavior but guards against its eradication. In other words, alternating between kindness and cruelty has the same effect as a Las Vegas slot machine. Sometimes it pays off, and sometimes it doesn't. You end up feeling exhilarated in the payoff no matter how little it might be, but over the long haul, you will lose. Secondly, the longer the cycles of intermittent reinforcement of reward, the stronger the traumatic bond and the more resistant to change it becomes. Guilt is the third issue. His behavior would set me on a guilt trip as I would be furious at him when he was mean, only to have him switch to Mr. Nice Guy. I remember talking to my classmates at the time, who lived in the projects and were dealing with some heavy stuff. I would think about my situation where I had a roof over my head and food to eat, but I was "unhappy" for some reason. When you are not getting beaten and have no scars or bruises, or not facing eviction, or worrying about your parents beating each other to a pulp, it seems so wrong to complain. As a child of a narcissist, you're incapable of pinning

---

14. "Brainwashing," accessed January 8, 2013, changingminds.org/techniques/conversion/brainwashing.htm, page 1.

15. Bonchay, Bree, "Narc-sadistic Brainwashing: The 8 Ingredients of Mind Control," accessed March 10, 2016, http://relationshipedia.me/2015/07/10/narc-sadistic-brainwashing-the-8-ingredients-of-mind- control/, pages 7–8.

down or labeling what's wrong, so you inevitably come to the conclusion that something must be wrong with you.

When you become an adult and your partner shows kindness after being abusive, this can become an addictive pattern (as mentioned previously), as the victim keeps hoping for the "kind" perpetrator to return. Domestic violence victims have told me numerous times how their abusers started off being the "ideal partner." They were exactly what they dreamed they would be like (i.e., their knights in shining armor), and that even though they became increasingly abusive, they remained ever hopeful that one day, this ideal partner would return. He never did. Commonly called the "cycle of violence"—a three-stage cycle consisting of (1) a buildup of tension, (2) abuse/battering, and (3) making up. Although some researchers believe there is no such thing as the abuse and kindness are often completely unpredictable. The pattern of pain followed by kindness was, however, found to lead to a "paradoxical attachment to the abuser." Also known as identification with the aggressor, or the Bettelheim Syndrome (which referred to concentration camp inmates who coped by identifying with their guards in hopes of survival). [16]

The Stockholm Syndrome also exemplified similar behavior (as after a bank robbery that involved many hostages, one woman later became engaged to one of the criminals and another developed a legal fund to aid in their criminal defense fees).

When I look back at my marriage, I would describe it as highly unpredictable and unstable due to the mixed messages of love and cruelty, and the constant criticism. When I was deep in the middle of it (I was relentless in my efforts to please my ex-husband), I completely lost any sense of which way was up. At the beginning of the relationship, I was idealized, and then never good enough. To top everything else, he blamed me for the change in him! I found myself in another prison

---

16. Mega, Lesly Tamarin; Mega, Jessica Lee; Mega, Benjamin Tamarin; and Harris, Beverly Moore, Brainwashing and Battering Fatigue, Psychological Abuse in Domestic Violence, NCMJ, vol. 61, no. 6 (September/October 2000).

with someone who wasn't in love with me. He was in love with control and the absolute power it gave him, made him heady. For the child of a narcissist who grows up to be in an abusive relationship with another narcissist, s/he has merely transferred from one prison growing up to yet another. She has already been conditioned and groomed for an imprisoned life where she is psychologically, emotionally, and sometimes physically tortured because it is all she has ever known. In other words, she has no idea of what it is like to be in a "healthy relationship." To be treated with respect and equality would likely seem alien to her, not to mention boring. She is already accustomed to living in a war zone, riding the roller-coaster ride of drama, and is addicted to the chemical rush that comes with never knowing what to expect.

When I examined my broken marriage in hindsight, and as I spoke with many domestic violence victims, I began to suspect that there was yet another plausible reason abused women refused to leave their abusive partners. I believe that in each consecutive relationship they became involved in, on some unconscious and primitive level, hope would spring eternal that this time, they would succeed in satisfying their current partner. The reason being they are locked into the maddening machinery that drives them to rework their failed relationship with their caregiver(s) via their relationships with each consecutive partner.

CHAPTER 6

GUILT, BLAME, AND SELF-LOATHING

The overwhelming sense of guilt and shame that a prisoner feels will cause him to be confused. The multiple accusations and assaults on his identity will cause him to lose—what, specifically, he is guilty of, and just feel the heavy burden of being wrong. This confusion allows the authorities to redirect the guilt toward whatever they please. Typically, the captors will accuse the prisoner of having lived a life of corruption and ascribing to a false ideology. Criticism and self-criticism are mechanisms of Communist thought control. In brainwashing, after a sufficient amount of guilt has been generated in the individual, sharing and self-criticism permit relief. The price paid for this relief, however, is loss of individuality and increased dependency.[17]

Guilt continues to be a mechanism that my parents use at will. They so excel at using it I have yet to wrap my head around exactly how they do it. I can certainly relate to the prisoner's experience of confusion, accusation, and just feeling the heavy burden of being wrong.

Perhaps it is because I already have instilled within me the propensity to be wrong; the predisposition of guilt already exists. Like the captor, my parents can simply redirect my guilt toward whatever they want. Having said that, it's worth taking some time to consider the level of shame you feel when you are constantly being accused and assaulted even though you don't understand why. It's the general feeling that you are just "bad." Author and therapist Alice Miller put it this way: "Many

---

17. *Declassified*, page 6.

people suffer all their lives from this oppressive feeling of guilt, the sense of not having lived up to their parents' expectations. This feeling is stronger than any intellectual insight they might have—that it is not a child's task or duty to satisfy his parents' needs. No argument can overcome these guilt feelings for they have their beginnings in life's earliest period, and from that, they derive their intensity and obduracy."[18]

I have to openly wonder here if, like the prison guards, my parents planted sufficient amounts of guilt within me so that I was essentially primed to replace myself with a "false self" of their making. My guilt would then become somewhat assuaged by embracing this foreign version of me. Of course, the price paid for this would be the loss of myself and increased dependency on my parents.

I believe I began feeling bad about myself as an infant. I remember getting furious at myself because my needs were getting in the way of taking care of my mother's needs (I was terrified I had overwhelmed her, which meant that my needs wouldn't be met). As a result, instead of tending to me, she placed me on the floor and walked away. I felt so helpless, frustrated, and trapped as I wasn't able to walk yet. I was disgusted with myself for being so needy. I think it was at this point that I realized I could discard the parts of myself that I despised in order to survive. There was a *M*A*S*H* episode[19] that clearly illustrated this brutal concept. Hawkeye (the lead character) and some Korean villagers were hiding from the enemy who had infiltrated the camp. One of the villagers was a mother, and her baby kept crying, threatening to reveal them. Hawkeye glanced disapprovingly at the mother who spontaneously broke the neck of the child. Hawkeye suffered a mental breakdown as a result. As horrible as the mother's action was, I understood her implicitly. It was all about survival.

When a child of a narcissist grows up and the threat of control is no longer a factor, the cost of survival becomes more evident. The

---

18. Miller, *Drama*, page 73.

19. "Goodbye, Farewell and Amen." *M*A*S*H*." Directed by Alan Alda, season 11, episode 16 (256 overall). Twentieth Television, February 28, 1983.

primary issue is that the self has been completely overshadowed by the narcissistic parents. This being the case, the child's parents never valued or nurtured her for who she was, nor did they invest any time in getting to know her. Consequently, as an adult, she will likely develop a strong proclivity to fill the empty void within her with a controlling, narcissistic partner. Thus, part of the healing process will involve her finding out who she is and reintegrating the parts of herself that she had tossed aside and sacrificed at the altar of survival.

I suffered from tremendous guilt as a child. I remember as a kid I showed my souvenirs to my cousins. I had purchased them during a family trip to Southern California. My mother put a massive guilt trip on me for doing this. I was confused and couldn't, for the life of me, figure out what I had done wrong. I ended up trying to give all my souvenirs away to my cousins because I felt so awful. They refused to take them though. My therapist explained to me that my mother's reaction had more to do with her than with me, as she probably felt guilty for not bringing souvenirs back for my cousins. This has turned out to be a truth that repeated itself as I tried to make sense of the confusing situations I found myself in as a child. It wasn't about me; it was about them. Narcissists rarely, if ever, take responsibility for their behavior. For the narcissistic parent, a child is a convenient receptacle to fill up with blame. You are blamed for nearly everything, including the abusive behavior of your parents.

To this day, if I am accused of something, I automatically consider the possibility that I am responsible. Continuous blaming tends to make a child feel inherently wrong and not worthy of being treated well. We are attracted to what is familiar—it breeds comfort. Although not everything that is comfortable is healthy. Consider the plight of women in abusive relationships who grew up in abusive homes. It is likely, for them, just more of the same.

CHAPTER 7

THE BEGINNINGS OF BRAIN FOG—TWISTED COMMUNICATION, SUBTLE COERCIVE CONTROL

One of the inherent rules in mind control is that you are not allowed to question anything the guard says. You quickly learn you have no voice: as even if you did somehow manage to say something, it inevitably falls on deaf ears. For a child of a narcissist, this is a set up for relentless and perpetual emotional abuse.

Wikipedia defined a "double bind" as an *anguish producing predicament in communication in which an individual (or group) receives two or more conflicting messages (or levels of communication), in which one message negates the other.* This creates a situation in which responding successfully to one message results in a failed response to the other (and vice versa) so that the person will be automatically wrong regardless of response. The double bind occurs when the person is restricted from metacommunicating (communicating about the communication or dilemma) and is unable to resolve it or get out of the situation.[20]

Gregory Bateson, who first described the double bind in the 1950s, added that double binds are often used as a covert form of coercion. The use of confusion makes them difficult to respond to or resist.[21] Wikipedia gives a classic example of a double bind: "that of a mother saying to her child that she loves her/him while turning away in contempt." The

20. "Double Bind," accessed October 14, 2013, www.en.m.wikipedia.org, page 1.
21. Bateson, G., "Steps to an Ecology of the Mind: a Revolutionary Approach to Man's Understanding of Himself," *Double Bind, 1969* (Chicago: University of Chicago Press, 1972), pages 271–278.

conflict caused by the incongruent messages of what is said vs. body language causes extreme anxiety due to the child's dependence on the mother. Her having to contend with contradictions and the fact that the child can neither ignore nor leave the relationship is due to her dependence on the parents for survival.

As I grew more aware of my feelings, they would often shed light onto things I had brushed off in the past. The birthday and Christmas cards I received from my parents would riddle me with guilt because they were so intimate and loving. I came to realize that the reason they upset me so was that the cards did not represent my experience at all. The conflict caused by incongruent messages, though subtle, caused me a great deal of confusion, distress, and guilt even after I left home.

Another example of a double bind would be an incident that took place when I was in elementary school. A male classmate had given me a white box, which appeared to be a gift. Inside was a dead spider. My teacher apparently called my father (I had been unaware of this), so the three of us (absent the teacher) were in the empty playground talking. At first, my father defended me and got down on the boy. I was so excited. I thought finally, my father was going to protect me and be a real father. I was completely mistaken. He quickly turned on me and said, "Why did you even take the box? I had to leave work early to come here!" I was so confused. Even though the boy had done something wrong to me, I was wrong for accepting the box. The underlying message was that I was not worth the time and money it took for him to advocate for me. In other words, I was a bother and an imposition for him.

There are four variations of the double bind.[22] The first and probably the most frequently used is what he calls the "be spontaneous" paradox. The wife who wants her husband to surprise her with flowers is experiencing this sort of dilemma. She is asking him to do something,

---

22. Guillaume, Patricia, "The Double Bind: The Intimate Tie between Behavior and Communication," accessed April 23, 2008, www.abusesanctuary.blogspot.com, page 3.

which by its nature, must be spontaneous. "It is one of the shortcomings of human communication that there is no way in which the spontaneous fulfillment of a need can be elicited from another person without creating this kind of self-defeating paradox," says Watzlawick.

A second variation of the double bind is *punishing the victim for a correct perception of the outside world.* The result of such a process is that the child learns to bypass her/his own perceptions in favor of her/his parent. For example, as a child, I saw my father lying on the grass, face down. I asked, "What's wrong with Dad?" My mother responded nonchalantly, "Oh, he's just taking a nap." In reality, he was drunk. With repeated parental corrections, I learned not to trust my own perceptions. This ultimately heightened my dependence on my parents. As an adult, it also made independent decision-making arduous and nearly impossible. Another side effect was not being able to trust my gut instinct, which I had learned from my parents to override. As an adult, my ability to protect myself by picking up on red flags within my environment was nonexistent, making me vulnerable to unseemly characters, predators, and other narcissists.

A third version of the double bind is *when a child is expected to have feelings other than those he experiences.* For example, my dad and I went on a bike ride; before he rode ahead of me and disappeared (to show how virile he was), he told me he would return. Well, I waited and kept riding for what seemed like an eternity until I finally stopped and began sobbing uncontrollably. Shortly after this, my father suddenly biked into view. He looked at me, unmoved by my tears, and said, "Why are you crying? I told you I would be back." I stopped in mid-sob because I was confused. I thought about it and realized he was right. When I brought up the incident in therapy (an attempt at clearing my brain fog), my therapist said, "Your father wasn't able to handle your crying so he pushed you away." Taking this a step further, I would dare to venture that he wanted to avoid looking like a bad parent to people passing by; I later discovered, narcissists are radically obsessed with maintaining a positive image. This sort of perverted communication happened to me so many times it left my head spinning, hence the long-term brain fog. I ended up feeling like someone had violently grabbed me by the throat, forcefully repressing many deep-seated sobs.

The fourth variation occurs *when a parent demands and restricts at the same time.* An example is when a parent demands honesty while encouraging winning at any cost. Thus, the child is placed in a bind where he has to disobey in order to obey.

In 1987 researchers discovered that the working element of a double bind is its pattern of disqualification. It is the means by which one person's experience is invalidated or dismissed as a result of an imposed bind. The four methods are as follows: *evasion, sleight of hand, literalization, and disqualification.*[23]

Evasion is a change of subject, where the previous statement does not clearly end a topic of discussion, and the next statement does not acknowledge the change in topic. Therefore, the second statement disqualifies the first.

For example, the incident with my father in which I ended up crying could be considered an example of evasion. I was expressing my concern that he failed to return for a long time, which made me afraid that he had abandoned me. I wasn't finished, but he changed the subject to what he had told me originally.

The second method of disqualification is *sleight of hand.* It occurs when the second response answers the first but changes the content of the first statement. This happened to me a lot. A general example was when I tried to communicate with my father about a concern; he would respond by giving some minimal acknowledgement and then completely change the subject. It was like magic—as if I had never said a thing—because the focus went quickly back to him.

The third type is *literalization.* It happens when the content of the previous statement is switched to a literal level in the next statement

---

23. Guillaume, *The Double Bind*, pages 3–4.

without acknowledgement of the change in structure. In some ways, the incident I had with my father (mentioned previously) is also an example of literalization. The focus shifted from my being upset that he was absent for so long, to the exact words he had spoken earlier, with no acknowledgement of the fact that I was in tears.

The fourth method of *status disqualification* occurs when a person uses personal status or superior knowledge to suggest that the previous message is not valid. For example, when I matriculated from graduate school, my mother ended up talking with a clinical psychology professor who had been responsible for organizing events for the Hawaii club. My mother asked me (with the professor looking on), "Why didn't you participate in the events?" I said, "I didn't have time. I was busy studying." My mother repeated the question, and I repeated my answer. It was as if my answer didn't even matter because the purpose of the conversation was for her to harangue me with the professor observing (so she could feel superior to me and better about herself, also known as narcissistic feeding).

I compare these four methods to the distraction a magician creates with his hands so you are diverted, incapable of realizing what is really going on. Narcissists are masters at manipulation and creating confusion for the express purpose of either keeping the focus off themselves, or exerting their superiority or both.

So what happens to a child who has to deal with these types of perverted interactions on a daily basis? An example of a case study: what happened to a hapless dog who was trained to discriminate between a circle and an ellipse, and then became unable to discriminate when the ellipse gradually expanded to look more like a circle. In a sense, this Pavlovian experiment had all the ingredients of a double bind, and the subsequent behavioral effects were actually called *experimental neurosis*. The dog was thus cast into a world where his survival depended on compliance with a law that violates itself. The dog manifested typical behavioral disorders; he could become comatose or viciously violent besides displaying physiological effects that were naturally associated with severe anxiety.[24]

Being exposed to this level of skewed miscommunication is akin to living in a war zone. The child is faced with the dilemma of trying desperately to figure out to which part of the message she can safely respond to. Much of our ability to make sense of the world depends on being able to recognize and comment upon the conflicting messages we receive—something a child of a narcissist is absolutely restricted from doing. Faced with the daunting task of deciphering the meaning of another's communication, while simultaneously being prohibited from commenting on it or acknowledging her own confusion, is a terrifying proposition.[25] Personally, I have no recollection of ever being anxiety-free, or having my basic needs of safety, security, and acceptance met while growing up. Relationships became as treacherous for me as walking through a minefield. When you are restricted from recognizing and discussing the conflicting messages coming at you, every communication becomes a threat to your personal safety. The options you have are quite sparse and most are merely a means of survival.

Obsessive anxiety. Faced with the refutable absurdity of her situation, a child will likely conclude that she must be overlooking vital clues either inherent in the situation or offered her by significant others (never considering the fact that what she is searching for may be deliberately withheld). She would be more prone to consider the later assumption, except for the fact that the others adamantly deny that anything about the situation is out of the ordinary. In either case—and this is the central issue—she will be obsessed with the need to find these clues. In order to give meaning to what is going on in and around her, she will eventually be driven to scan for clues and meaning in the most unlikely and unrelated areas. This focus away from the real issues is all the more

---

24. Watzlawick, Paul; Beavin Bavelas, Janet; Jackson, Don D., *Pragmatics of Human Communication: A Study of Interactional Patterns, Pathologies, and Paradoxes* (New York, NY: W. W. Norton & Company Inc., 1967), pages 217–218.

25. Guillaume, *The Double Bind*, page 6.

plausible if one is reminded that the essential ingredient of a double bind is restricting the awareness of the contradictions involved.[26] I have to wonder if my honed ability to analyze and figure out what might have caused a client's mental illness has something to do with having to forge this skill early in life.

Emotional deprivation. Studies of controlled starvation indicate that the entire value system of the subjects underwent a change. Bottom line was that their level of irritation increased while their ability to think clearly decreased.

The author Roald Dahl described how the main character Charlie Bucket (a young child) learned to manage his hunger and starvation. When I read *Charlie and the Chocolate Factory,* I was a child myself, and I was struck by how he so accurately and poignantly described what it was like to starve (even though my starvation was emotional rather than physical). He wrote, "And now, very calmly, with the curious wisdom that seems to come so often to small children in times of hardship, he began to make little changes here and there in some of the things that he did, so as to save his strength. In the mornings, he left the house ten minutes earlier so that he could walk slowly to school, without ever having to run. He sat quietly in the classroom during break, resting himself, while the others rushed outdoors and threw snowballs and wrestled in the snow. Everything he did now, he did slowly and carefully, to prevent exhaustion."[27]

I had incorporated many of the things Charlie Bucket did to conserve my emotional strength. I was so emaciated emotionally that when people showed me any attention or kindness of any sort, I wanted to follow them home. I believe my emotional deprivation made me an easy target for sexual abuse. As my child-self said, "When I got molested, they focused on getting what they wanted from me. I had their attention like I never got from my parents. But they weren't looking at me. They never

26. Watzlawick, *Pragmatics,* page 218.
27. Dahl, R., *Charlie and the Chocolate Factory* (NY.: A. A. Knopf, 1964) 23.

looked at me. They acted like they cared about me, but they wanted my body, not me." Still, for a long time, I clung to the attention I received from the abuse like a child clings to her security blanket because it was the closest I got to being loved (perverted as it was). Metaphorically speaking, I was so emotionally starved I was willing to eat food that was obviously tainted with poison.

In hindsight, I believe the emotional abuse I experienced during childhood became especially evident when I began therapy, as what I lacked was brought to light by what my therapist encompassed. I felt delight with the lilt in her voice as I was used to the monotone, lifeless voices of my parents. She was responsive to me in her facial expressions, when I was accustomed to the blank look on my parents' faces. I couldn't believe that my therapist was really happy to see me during each session because I was used to being ignored or treated as an imposition or bother. I was worried she might become disgusted with me; I would be too much for her to handle. Even worse, I would somehow lose her. In the past, love was taken away, and I failed to live up to my parents' demands. Rejection and abandonment became the norm for me. Grasping for relationship with my therapist was a huge risk. The fear of losing her plagued me for a long time.

Cognitive dissonance. It is defined as a distressing feeling caused by holding conflicting ideas simultaneously.[28] Hearing that it is okay and not okay to do something would create conflict and confusion. Cognitive dissonance proposes that people have a motivational drive to reduce dissonance by adjusting themselves: changing beliefs, attitudes, and actions.

Dissonance can also be reduced by making excuses: justifying, blaming, and denying. For me, it was somewhat helpful to keep telling myself that "how I felt didn't matter." I used to cry about everything as

---

28. Monika, "Blinded, Bound, and Burdened: Parental Alienation and Two Theories—the Double Bind & Cognitive Dissonance," accessed October 14, 2013, www.parentalalienationsupport.com, page 3.

a child, and repeating this statement hardened me until I actually began to believe it was true.

Blind obedience. Obedience is the path of least resistance, which is of primary importance when you're dealing with a narcissist. For the narcissist, it's always "my way or the highway." Like military recruits who quickly determine that in the face of bewildering logic, or lack thereof, in military life, that the best possible response is to comply implicitly and literally (and to refrain from any independent thinking).[29] I chose to do the same.

I recall one incident where I was on another bike ride with my dad. We were stopped at a major intersection. I could have sworn I heard him say, "Go!" Even though I knew it wasn't our turn, I overrode my minimally functioning gut instinct and went through the intersection alone. There was a police officer present, but thankfully, he did nothing. As you can imagine, I was reprimanded and I felt so ashamed. I wonder though if his criticism of me had more to do with him feeling embarrassed by my behavior in the public eye, than anything else.

Allow me to veer off on a tangent here. If you were raised in a home where you were threatened covertly and overtly, not allowed to question, clarify, and/or discuss what was said, it would make sense that you would be attracted to people similar to your parents/caregivers. It is comfortably familiar, and you are accustomed to being treated in such a manner, as you don't know anything else. In other words, being treated with respect would be considered foreign to you. My theory is that prior to becoming involved with abusive men/women, domestic violence victims already have a predisposition for being abused. Somewhere in their childhood, if you dug deep enough, you would most likely find a narcissist who had already done the groundwork: preparing the victim for a lifetime of abuse. Many theorists miss the full context, as they fail to take into account the victims' upbringing.

Learned helplessness and withdrawing from human interaction. Learned helplessness is a psychological paralysis exhibited by caged dogs subjected to

29. Watzlawick, *Pragmatics*, page 218.

electrical shocks at random and varied intervals. At first, the dogs tried to escape but eventually became despondent after realizing they were powerless to do anything about their predicament. In subsequent situations in which escape or avoidance was possible, the dogs failed to take action.[30]

Battered women, POWs, battle-fatigued soldiers, and children of narcissists often experience a form of learned helplessness due to their inability to escape or change their situation.[31] Physical and emotional mistreatment lead to exhaustion, and a reduced ability to reason and resist. A feeling of helplessness in the face of the impersonal machinery of control is carefully cultivated within the prisoner where he not only begins to feel like an animal but feels that nothing can be done about it. Through his strictly enforced regiment, no one pays attention to him or listens to his complaints. He experiences isolation, and having lost nearly all communication, he begins to feel that he has been forgotten.[32]

For me, learned helplessness lead to depression and fantasies of lying in a coffin and wishing I were dead. I envied people who had died. I longed for death the way people hunger for food. Death seemed to be the only way out, and I wanted out so badly.

Withdrawing from human contact can be achieved by physically isolating oneself as much as possible and blocking any channels of communication where isolation is not possible to the desired extent. Such a person would appear withdrawn, unapproachable, and autistic.[33]

For me, withdrawing represented a means of self-preservation. Blending into the wallpaper helped me to somewhat avoid becoming a victim of my father's unpredictable rages. Being emotional was the equivalent of painting a target sign on myself, so I tried my best to keep my emotions under wraps. This usually meant going numb.

30. L. Nolan, Jeannette. "Learned Helplessness," accessed December 18, 2018, www.britannica.com/science/learned-helplessness, pages 1–2.

31. Mega, *Brainwashing and Battering*, page 262.

32. *Declassified*, Page 8.

33. Watzlawick, *Pragmatics*, page 218.

Withdrawing brought with it some other concurrent problems, though, such as crippled social skills. In elementary school, my classmates told me, "You don't know how to talk to people." I was horrified and immediately began working on improving my communication/ interaction skills. Since I had such a poor example in my parents (they fought a lot when I was younger), I took it upon myself to make the necessary changes. I also had the problem of being incredibly shy. Once when I had to present a book report, my teacher decided she was going to help me overcome my shyness. She told me to say something positive about myself, something I don't even remember. After saying it, I burst into tears in front of the class. Although she meant well, my teacher inevitably made things worse for me. On a side note, I continue to struggle with my ability to project my voice when I need to speak publicly because my voice sounds loud in my own head. I'm unable to gauge how it sounds to others. Interestingly enough, some domestic violence victims reported having the same problem. I suppose once you become the wallpaper, it's difficult to reverse the process.

Recently, I also discovered children of narcissists shared the problem of being incapable of breathing deeply. I assume when you're living in chaos, it's a given that your breathing will be shallow due to stress.

The struggle to have a voice and hold on to my own opinions. When I was a teenager, I came home excited about the movie *Billy Jack*[34] which I had just seen. The lead character Billy Jack was played by Tom Laughlin. I am guessing in hindsight here that I liked the movie because he was a rebel, he protected the vulnerable; and when dealing with bullies, he would clearly tell them what he was going to do to them before he did it.

Unfortunately for them, they would foolishly brush off his warning in disbelief and paid the consequences afterward. I was gushing with feelings and thoughts about it. My father did not share my youthful enthusiasm and instead, redirected my focus on a movie he believed

---

34. *Billy Jack*, Directed by Tom Laughlin. Performances by Tom Laughlin and Delores Taylor. National Student Film Corporation, 1971.

was worthy of accolades. He got me to think like he did about an actress whom he felt had excelled in her performance. My father went on to explain why he felt this way. I had no recollection of what I had been excited about earlier, until I got more in touch with my feelings.

I have no problem, however, remembering what my father said. Being routinely coerced into thinking like he did made it challenging for me as an adult to hold on to my own opinions/beliefs. I realize this is an ability most people take for granted, but brainwashing creates profound difficulties that the average person will never have to address. When faced with challenges to my opinion, it's as if my opinion begins to evaporate immediately upon hearing someone else's. It's as if I hear another's opinion, their opinion begins to seep into my head against my will and there's nothing I can do to resist it. As a result, I start questioning my belief in favor of theirs.

Nowadays, I'm able to hold on to my opinions a bit longer than I used to, but I almost have to isolate myself to do so (so I don't hear others' opinions). As mentioned in the foreword, it was as if there was no place my child-self could hide from her father because he would drill himself into her brain; at that age, there was nothing she could do to defend herself.

I identified with one of the guest characters on the *Alias* series[35] programed to kill; he was beginning to unravel. Instead of seeing the murders he committed in black and white so he could dissociate, he started to have nightmares in vivid color. As the lead character Sydney Bristow began to put the pieces back together for him, he spoke about how terrified he was that he might actually be a killer. He said he had voluntarily admitted himself to a mental institution, just in case he was. After Sydney helped him escape, she learned that he was responsible for killing her fiancé. She also realized they both were being used by an agency falsely claiming to be a part of the CIA (SD6). In a moment of angst, he said, "I don't know if there ever was a me."

---

35. "Reckoning," *Alias*, Directed by Daniel Attias, season 1, episode 6. Buena Vista Television, November 18, 2001.

His statement has stayed with me for years because I constantly ask the same question. When you've been brainwashed, it almost goes without saying that you have to wonder if there ever was a *me*—a pristine, untouched, unpolluted *me*. Then you spend the rest of your life getting de-programed so you can find *her.*

The terrorizing fear of being overwhelming that results in abandonment. The child of a narcissist is constantly in a precarious situation where she needs to focus on taking care of the needs of her parents in hopes that she will get some of her needs met as well. The problem is her needs continue increasing exponentially due to rarely being met, but she must keep this issue under wraps; otherwise she will become too much for her parents. The danger is if her heightened needs are exposed, this will result in abandonment and/or rejection.

Additionally, when she is unable to meet the impossible standards set by her parents, this also results in abandonment. For me, this pattern had persisted since I was an infant; by the time I got older, I was a nervous, crying child who probably triggered my parents to no end because of my neediness. I was convinced that my parents were going to abandon me at the biggest shopping mall in Hawaii where it would be easier to lose me. When I told my mother about my fear, she just laughed and told me I was ridiculous to think such a thing. Nevertheless, every time we went to the mall, I was in a panic, trying to figure out how I would ever get home should they choose to abandon me.

Another thing that aggravated my abandonment issues was the way my mother would kick me out of the car and drive off when she didn't like what I said. She would drive ahead of me and then come back to pick me up. I always refused at first. My brother did the same thing when we had an argument. As an adult, I seemed to repeat this pattern of attaching to people who didn't want to be around me. I refer to this as the "unwanted barnacle syndrome". I guess barnacles tend to be unwanted anyway, but my emphasis here is that this is a double negative. You're not wanted for who you are, and you're not wanted by the people you chose to attach to. What ultimately ended up happening repeatedly was I would keep trying to hold on to the relationship while the other person was doing their best to scrape me off and end it. I would keep trying to make them happy (whether it was my ex-husband or a friend), hoping that my efforts would eventually be rewarded or at the least appreciated, but they rarely were.

It bears mentioning for clarity's sake that for the child of a narcissistic parent, her needs are a liability and a viable threat to her existence because she is dependent on her parents for survival. For the narcissistic parents, the child's needs are a bother and an imposition because they get in the way of them fulfilling their own needs. The narcissist is governed by his or her feelings while the decent person is governed by his or her obligations. Since a narcissistic parent is governed by his or her feelings and lacks any empathy, they are unable to own up to their obligations to shield their child from emotional heartache.[36]

You are unwittingly drafted and recruited for the job of protecting your abused parent, and this often evolves into your real job as an adult. I've spoken to other children of narcissists who shared similar experiences. As a child, you are sucked into defending/protecting your abused/abusing parent; and as an adult, your job seems to morph into something where you fight endlessly against injustice. Giving and fighting endlessly, it seems we have been conditioned and wired this way. Really, it's not a bad thing. In fact, it can be a good thing. Being involved in helping people is certainly culturally reinforced, for women especially.

Nevertheless, there are three problems inherent in giving and fighting endlessly. First, is this really what you want, or are you so deeply hardwired that you actually don't know? Sometimes you have to get off the hamster wheel to find out. Second, endlessly giving and/or fighting can lead to exhaustion and burnout. This tendency to put your needs last combined with giving and fighting ad nauseam is a set up for disaster. Third, why must the giving and/or fighting be endless? You now have

---

36. Prager, Dennis, "Brainwashing Children, Narcissistic Parents," accessed February 7, 2012, www.brainwashingchildren.com/2011/01/the-narcissistic-parent/, page 2.

the power to set boundaries on how much and how far you will go. Additionally, if you are in the situation where you are giving to people who appear entitled to receive (nothing seems to be enough, and they never express any appreciation), you are in a setup to be drained dry.

When you've been programmed to give/fight endlessly, it will take some effort to stop and change. Otherwise, you end up spending your life living for others at the expense of yourself.

You may be praised for being so selfless, but is it really selfless-ness when you've been conditioned to behave that way? The praise of others becomes a kind of food for you because it's the closest you'll get to being able to build up your shriveled self-esteem. Being a people pleaser magnifies this hunger to another level, making it potentially addictive. I'd like to expand on this issue a bit. I've met many domestic violence victims who have spent years pouring their lives into others and were living vicariously through them. When I asked them what they dreamed about for themselves, they usually responded with a blank stare and/or had to think really hard to come up with an answer. The majority of these women had put their dreams on hold for so long they had to be dusted off. Part of the healing process involved breathing life into these dreams again. I remind them you were placed on this earth for a special purpose. There are things that were planned for you to do and no one else.

Systematic humiliation/contempt, narcissistic feeding, and implanted cruelty. In order to hasten the deterioration of prisoners' sense of values and resistance, other methods of control were used in combination with the basic processes. These included humiliation.

Prisoners were often humiliated by having to soil themselves as they were prohibited from using toilet facilities. Others were restricted from bathing for weeks until they felt despicable.[37] For the child of a narcissist, the process of being humiliated and treated with contempt is called narcissistic feeding. The child's parents (who are like giants in

---

37. *Declassified*, page 6.

her eyes and with whom she is no match) will either work in tandem, or individually, to find ways of using their strength and superiority to shame and despise the child. As Alice Miller explained, "[my parents] encountered their own humiliating past in my eyes, and they warded it off with the power they now had. My suffering was accentuated by my parents' demonstrating their grown-upness to avenge themselves unconsciously on me for their earlier humiliation."[38]

This behavior repeats itself over and over because narcissists need to feed, and their children are easily accessible and unable to escape. Here's an example: As a child, I accidentally swallowed an apple seed while eating an apple. I was terrified that the seed would grow in my stomach. I ran to tell my mother what had happened. She said, "Yes, it's going to grow in your stomach, and then it's going to get bigger and grow through your head." I was shocked and gasped at her response. After a moment passed, she began to laugh, then told me the truth that I would be all right. I was at a loss to understand why my own mother would respond in such a way, especially when she saw my face and knew how distressed I was. Narcissistic feeding would explain her behavior.

As an adult, I worked on the frontlines in mental health, fighting injustice and cruelty; but within, I harbored my childhood experiences of cruelty and contempt. Because I wasn't in touch with my feelings, I would unconsciously inflict similar cruelty on weaker adults with whom I was acquainted (they reminded me of my mother). I remember despising how weak they were, just like my father would despise my mother. I think for me, this was the purest example of brainwashing because being cruel to anyone was so unfamiliar to me. Yet, it felt as if these motives had been implanted in my brain by a programmer. I was appalled that I was capable of behaving like my father especially when I knew what it felt like to be on the receiving end. When we don't address our experiences and pain, we run the risk of creating generational damage. I believe this was the main reason God wouldn't allow me to have children.

---

38. Miller, *Drama*, page 87.

Reaching empty. For the brainwashing process to be successful, the prisoner does not consciously change his value system, rather the change occurs *despite* his efforts. Under the imposition of the internal conflict aroused by guilt, his weakened mind "going blank" for longer periods of time, and the threat of a potential breakdown, he agrees to write a confession. Every sentence is questioned by the interrogator, who edits the confession with the prisoner. The prisoner is forced to argue against each and every change. This is the essence of brainwashing. The prisoner, desperate to maintain some semblance of integrity and avoid further brainwashing, begins to accept as his own the statements he has written, using the interrogator's own arguments to support his position. Through this process, identification with the interrogator's value system becomes complete even though the prisoner is oblivious to the transition.[39]

For me, the obvious power differential between me and my parents meant that my efforts to fight back were minimal and easily crushed. I was forced to create a "false self" that was more like the "me" they wanted and approved of. Unfortunately, they ended up rejecting my false self as well because even that "me" was not up to their standards. All I can say was that I felt lost for most of my adult life. I had the underlying sense that I was a shell of a person (there was no me at the core), but there was nothing I could really do about it mainly because I was so unaware. I will say that my abusive relationship with my ex-husband did work in a positive way to bring to the surface many of my issues.

There's something that happens to you when you give and give until there is nothing left. This happened to me while I was still living under my parents' roof. I tried to make them aware of this concern, but my cries fell on deaf ears. My anguish and shrouded rage were projected onto a couple in the news. They had decided to conceive a second child in hopes that her healthy organ(s) would be donated to save her sister when she got older. I found this so convoluted and unfair because the child was conceived for the express purpose set by her parents instead

---

39. *Declassified*, page 10.

of having her for being her. At the time, I felt, metaphorically speaking, that all my organs had been removed by my parents; I had nothing left to give them. This didn't seem to matter at all to them because their demands for giving more of myself never diminished one bit.

> There are people who have to pay for the smallest things in life with their very substance and their spinal cord. That is a constantly recurring pain. (Alphonse Dauder in *Lettres de mon Moulin*)

An absence of rage. I believe a major reason I seemed to express so little rage was because having any anger was dangerous, as my father was the one entitled to release his sudden angry tirades that terrorized the family like incoming missiles. You learn quickly not to do anything that rocks the boat.

Another reason for my lack of anger was I had learned to lock it up early as a child. I remember making sure I walked on all the cracks in the sidewalk on the way to school to ensure that my anger would be under control. While I was in therapy, I had quite a few vivid and thought-provoking dreams involving my anger. In one, I was beating up someone with a whip, whose back was facing me. When the person turned around to face me and make me stop, it turned out to be me. I was stunned. I realized I had turned my rage inward.

As I got deeper into therapy, I had a dream where I was in a kind of wildlife habitat, and vicious animals representing my feelings were on leashes. I was taking them to see my therapist, but I did so with much trepidation because I was terrified that I wouldn't be able to control them and they would end up tearing her apart.

Much later in therapy, I had a glimpse of my rage in the form of a dream. Ironically, as it turned out, it was a double bind situation. A man was on a pier facing me. I believe he represented my father. He looked strong and somewhat muscular. Behind him, a huge whale or fish was quickly approaching with its mouth wide open, as if ready to eat him.

My father was oblivious to this as he was focused on a sea turtle he had in his grip on the pier. He was about to kill it. I believe the sea turtle represented my child-self. I felt infuriated that my father was going to hurt the innocent sea turtle who had done nothing to him. The dilemma for me was whether to remain silent and let the whale/fish eat him so the turtle could be saved or warn my father and allow him to kill the turtle.

As I edged even closer to my rage during therapy, I kept drawing a screaming head in profile with a hand gripped tightly around its neck. Prior to this, when I was searching for something visual to better express what I was feeling, I came across a screaming head from Picasso's Guernica and found I had an affinity with it. Eventually, I came to realize that the screaming head represented me. All the screams of my past that I longed to release had been squelched, stuck in my throat for most of my life (because of the many double binds and manipulative communications I had experienced).

CHAPTER 8

THE INSIDIOUS EFFECTS OF EMOTIONAL ABUSE

"Emotional abuse is like brainwashing in that it systematically wears away at the victim's self-confidence, sense of self-worth, trust in their own perceptions, and self-concept."[40] The result is the victim's self-esteem becomes so low she clings to the abuser (she sides with the abuser as a survival tactic). The abuser, through relentless assaults on her self-esteem has managed to convince her that she is worthless and unwanted, so she remains in the abuse. Her all-consuming fear of being alone also keeps her immobilized.

I'd like to touch on this fear of being alone for a moment. This fear was very real for me when I was married to my ex-husband. I seemed to prefer being abused and miserable to being alone. In hindsight, I believe this desperation to avoid being alone had to do with the vast, deep pit of emptiness within my core as a child of a narcissist. I theorize that because the self was never allowed to fully develop, it is far easier to insert a person in that vacuum—one who is so full of themselves. They overwhelmingly distract you from the pain that is too immense to face. The totality of the torture the abuser inflicts on you doesn't even come close to the pain within you.

Abusive expectations. Domestic violence abusers often place unrealistic demands on the victim. They expect her to drop everything to tend to their needs. The bottom line is that no matter how much you do, it is never enough; for this, you are on the receiving end

---

40. Hein, Steve. "Emotional Abuse," accessed August 13, 2014, eqi/eabuse1.htm, pages 2–6.

of constant criticism. I've noticed while growing up and within my abusive marriage situation that narcissists often have a "prove you love me" attitude. They question and test your love and loyalty so they can manipulate you to do what they want. They say things like, "If you really loved me, you would do this for me." For the child of a narcissist, this challenge is what locks them on the hamster wheel of effort. They were on it growing up and now they find themselves back on it again. As it was in childhood, so it repeats itself in adulthood. It is hauntingly familiar. The abusers may have changed, but the results are the same—they are rarely, if ever, satisfied. The hidden truth buried under all the manipulation, confusion, and drama is this: they love torturing and controlling you much more than they actually love you. Have you noticed that the accusations are mainly one-sided? Eventually, victims withdraw from fighting back, due to brutal conditioning.

Aggressing. I noticed with domestic violence victims that their abusers were already in the habit of pointing an accusing finger at them. They had already stationed themselves in a one-up position so the victims were forced to constantly defend themselves. Aggressive abuse includes: accusation, blaming, threatening and ordering. It may be direct or indirect; taking on various forms that appear to be "helping" such as offering solutions or advising. Upon closer inspection, what appears to be "helping" is more like an attempt to belittle, control or demean. What unveils it is the judgmental "I know best" tone that works to create unequal footing rather than fostering the equality and autonomy necessary for healthy adult relationships. When I graduated from high school, I was desperate to be accepted anywhere, so I could find my place in the world. I hated the feeling of being out in the open and exposed. I actually considered becoming a carpenter in the army for the simple reason that I was thrilled they were willing to accept me. My father said this, "One day, you will find yourself building something and wishing you had listened to your father." I never joined the army.

In domestic violence relationships, nit-picking is an ambient form of aggressive abuse.[41] It's used to wear down the target as a defense mechanism to ward off the abuser's own feelings of inadequacy. His/her fault-finding efforts and accusations, while covertly disguised as helpful, are actually intended to make one believe they are inadequate, not good enough. What the abuser is looking for is a double-dose feeding—a boost of superiority for making one feel both inadequate and dependent. The noose tightens as dominance and control increase. Meanwhile, efforts to avoid conflict result in more and more concessions, which translate into the loss of yourself.

Constant chaos. My ex-husband was a rage-a-holic just like my father and my maternal grandfather. This equates to generations of unpredictable behavior. Growing up for me was chaotic because my parents were always fighting. I was reluctantly forced to witness the process of my father breaking down my mother until she had no will to fight back anymore. It is a sickening thing to watch. I would compare the experience to watching someone kick a puppy around.

Recent research into domestic violence shows that even a child in the womb can be impacted by domestic violence.[42] My younger brother ended up punching holes in the walls as an adolescent. I believe he was the pressure valve in our family that prevented us from exploding. The chaos in my marriage was something to behold. When I started seeing my therapist and began setting boundaries with my then husband, he lost it. Once, post explosion, he chased me on the freeway, riding my bumper all the way home. The twisted ramifications to all this insanity is that the victim will attach to her partner, as long as there is a high level of emotional intensity, good or bad. This explains one of the reasons why it is so hard for victims to leave their abusers. For me, the only, and I mean only, reason I left was because God told me to leave. It was a simple act of obedience. I believe he had had his fill of watching me

41. Bonchay, Narc-sadistic, page 8.
42. "Domestic Abuse May Affect Children in Womb," accessed December 6, 2018, zwww.sciencedaily.com/releases/2014/12/141216100628.htm, page 1.

be abused. Had I been left to my own devices, I would no doubt have remained with my ex-husband to this day.

Denying. It is a form of abuse where a child's emotional needs are denied. Especially when they need it the most. It is done with the express purpose of hurting, punishing, or humiliating. The abuser can deny a victim's perceptions, memory, and sanity. Withholding is a derivative of denying, which may include: refusing to listen, communicate, and withdrawing emotionally in the form of silent treatment. As a child, I was starving for attention and emotional sustenance. One day, I remember approaching my mother because I was excited and wanted to share something. She was buried in a newspaper or magazine and never looked up. "Later," she said.

I came up to her time and again, only to be brushed aside. Finally, after what seemed like an eternity to my child-self, she asked, "What did you want to talk to me about?" I told her, "Nothing. I forgot about it." In truth, I had not forgotten about it. I was resistant to give her any opportunity to redeem herself because I was too proud to put myself out there once more, unwilling to risk my last shreds of dignity. I never approached her this way again.

Denial is insidious in its ability to lower self-esteem and create conflict. But even more damage is caused by the constant invalidation of reality, feelings, and experiences. Here, denial works to erode confidence in your most important survival tool—your mind. *Gaslighting* is a domestic violence term used to describe the abusers' denial of the victims' perceptions, which works to rattle and jar their sanity. Narcissists tend to be chronic liars. They are so convinced of their own deceptions that they are capable of making you doubt yourself and your sanity even when you know you are right.

Dominating. When I was married to my ex-husband, he used the threat of divorce to control me for almost seven years. I remember one incident where I begged him not to divorce me. What struck me was his attitude when he responded. He agreed not to divorce me (for the moment anyway), but was nonchalant about it; as if he didn't care. I felt as if he was treating me with contempt. I subsequently lost all respect for myself. You could also refer to this incident as an example of *emotional blackmail,* as my ex-husband played on my fear of being alone/abandoned to gain control of me.

Invalidation. I believe at one point, I was an emotionally sensitive child, but being immersed in the toxic environment of my family changed everything. I am almost certain that having my feelings invalidated ad infinitum had something to do with this.

Invalidation to me is a deceptive form of control. It is often cloaked in helpfulness, but is very destructive. Allow me to explain: I believe simply opening up about how you feel almost automatically places you in a vulnerable position. Refusing to validate someone's feelings is like a slap in the face. It's as if the other person's feelings were too threatening or uncomfortable, so you tell them how they "should" feel instead.

When my family went to Disneyland with my young cousin and her family, everyone wanted to ride the Pirates of the Caribbean ride except her. She was terrified. My cousin didn't like the looks of the ride at all. I watched everyone invalidate her feelings so we could go on the ride together. She cried and cried through the whole thing because she was so scared. I felt so bad because I understood what it was like for her, and by watching her in distress, I felt as if I was reliving my own.

Minimizing. Minimizing is a less severe form of denial. The abuser may not deny that a particular event occurred, but the recipient's experience or reaction to the event is questioned. I was told many times that I was "too sensitive," or "it's all in your head." I hated it when my parents told me these things. I remember on one occasion, I decided that I wanted to spend time with my father by going running with him. He chose to go running at noon, which was an especially hot time in Hawaii. When I complained about the heat, he said, "it was all in my head, and that I should instead imagine I was absorbing the rays of the sun so I was invigorated like he was." The fact that running at noon was generally considered ill-advised was not even considered.

Such statements implied that my emotions and perceptions were faulty and shouldn't be trusted.

Trivializing. It is a more subtle form of minimizing and occurs when the abuser suggests that what you have done or communicated is inconsequential or unimportant. An example of this would be the way my father often competed with me when it came to graphic arts. I remember when I was in college, I did an oil pastel drawing of a boat at the pier for one of my assignments. I thought it came out pretty well. When he saw it, he pointed out a flaw—that I had drawn the wake of the boat inaccurately. He became much more competitive when I started attending Art Center College of Design for my undergraduate degree.

Unpredictable responses. An example which I believe took place within the same day. My ex was in a good mood and told me he was so happy to be married to me. Later in the day, when he became infuriated over something I had done, he demanded that I move out of the apartment immediately. His behavior was completely unpredictable, and I never knew what would set him off. You could say his behavior was reminiscent of my father in that respect. Thus, I was accustomed to being treated in this fashion.

I remember once when I was sitting quietly, reading a comic book on a train ride to Northern California and my father became enraged when he saw what I was doing. He yelled, "We paid all this money for this trip and you're going to read your comic book? You should be looking outside at the scenery!" I couldn't understand what I did wrong. I would parallel living with my father and my ex to living on the side of an active volcano. By the time I left my ex, I had a rash with oozing sores covering my scalp. Another rash nearly covered the rest of my body. I was afraid I was losing my mind and out of desperation sought out a therapist, something I would otherwise never have had the nerve to do.

When my ex and I were in couple's therapy, any examination of his responsibility in the relationship was pretty much brushed aside or locked up. His criticism of me became the endless focus of sessions, and I wrote all of his concerns down. As the sessions continued, I only saw the list get longer. It was then that it finally dawned on me that my marriage was over. I would consider this method a form of evasion or sleight of hand because what it did was maintain the focus on me (the victim) because the perpetrator was incapable of handling any form of criticism or self-evaluation.

Verbal assaults. Berating, belittling, criticizing, name-calling, screaming, threatening, excessive blaming, using sarcasm and humiliation. Blowing your flaws out of proportion and making fun of you in front of others. My father could bring my mother to tears with his verbal assaults. He also had the habit of making fun of her by blaming and using sarcasm. Once when we visited the other islands of Hawaii for our vacation, we were going to go out for a spin on some rented Motobécanes. My mother had some difficulty balancing herself, and my father made so much fun of her she cried and opted out of going with us. My ex-husband loved to prod and poke at me until I got upset so he could pick a fight with me. It was like a sport to him. He also had the ability to cut me to shreds with his words in a matter of seconds.

The look of disapproval. I wanted to add this because I can't count how many times my parents used this to control me. When you think about it, it's pretty amazing that you could control someone with just a look. Once when I came home from Chicago, I was wearing a black dress and leather belt, both of which I had purchased at Banana Republic. I thought I looked pretty good, but when they saw me, they gave me that look. I couldn't figure out why (notice how I have to constantly figure out and make meaning of their behavior) they disapproved of my outfit, especially since it was pretty conservative and was even pictured in the Banana Republic catalogue.

I'm gradually reaching the point where I don't care if they disapprove of me, but I've been so conditioned I know it's going to take time.

When I began therapy, I felt extremely concerned about my therapist's facial expressions even though she consistently appeared happy to see me. I think I was terrified of getting "the look." She never did look at me this way.

Quoted here are two adapted lists of characteristics of emotionally abused people (List One was based on Studies of Adult Children of Alcoholics, List Two was based on Recovery and Support Groups. Both are also relevant for children of narcissists).[43]

LIST ONE

- can only guess at what healthy behavior is

- have trouble completing things

- lie when they don't need to. Lying might have been a survival tactic in the home (perhaps the child learned from parents who lied to cover up problems or avoid conflict. Or simply to avoid harsh punishment, or to get needed attention. But as an adult, that tactic is no longer appropriate)

- judge themselves without mercy

- have trouble accepting compliments

- often take responsibility for problems, but not successes

- or they go to the other extreme and refuse to take any responsibility for mistakes while trying to take credit for the work of others

- have trouble having fun since their childhoods were lost, stolen, repressed

- take themselves very seriously or not seriously at all

- have difficulty with intimate relationships

- expect others to just "know what I want." (They can't express it because they were so often disappointed as children that they learned to stop asking for things)

- overreact to things beyond their control

---

43. Geringer Woititz, Janet. "List 1—Based on Studies of Adult Children of Alcoholics," accessed August 13, 2014, eqi.org/eabuse1/htm, 7–9.

- constantly seek approval and affirmation

- feel different from others

- Are extremely loyal even when facing overwhelming evidence that their loyalty is undeserved

- are either super responsible or super irresponsible

- tend to lock themselves into a course of action without giving serious consideration to alternative behaviors or possible consequences (this impulsiveness leads to confusion, self-loathing, and loss of control over their environment. The result is that they spend much energy blaming others, feeling victimized and cleaning up messes)

LIST TWO

- feelings of low self-esteem (they say as a result of being criticized)

- We perpetuate these parental messages by judging ourselves and others harshly. We try to cover up our poor opinions of ourselves by being perfectionistic, controlling, contemptuous, and gossipy.

- We tend to isolate ourselves out of fear, and we feel often uneasy around other people especially authority figures.

- We are desperate for love and approval and will do anything to make people like us. Not wanting to hurt others, we remain "loyal" in situations and relationships even when evidence indicates our loyalty is undeserved (not wanting to lose them, having an extremely hard time letting go.)

- We are intimidated by angry people and personal criticism. This causes us to feel inadequate and insecure (further adding to our feelings of inadequacy and insecurity).

- We continue to attract emotionally unavailable people with addictive personalities.

- We live life as victims, blaming others for our circumstances, and are attracted to other victims (and people with power) as friends and lovers. We confuse love with pity and tend to "love" people we can pity and rescue (and we confuse love with need).

- We are either super-responsible or super-irresponsible. We take responsibility for solving others' problems or expect others to be responsible for solving ours. This enables us to avoid being responsible for our own lives and choices.

- We feel guilty when we stand up for ourselves or act in our own best interests. We give in to others' needs and opinions instead of taking care of ourselves.

- We deny, minimize, or repress our feelings as a result of our traumatic childhoods. We are unaware of the impact that our inability to identify and express our feelings has had on our adult lives.

- We are dependent personalities who are so terrified of rejection or abandonment that we tend to stay in situations or relationships that are harmful to us. Our fears and dependency stop us from ending unfulfilling relationships and prevent us from entering into fulfilling ones (because we feel so unlovable that it is difficult or impossible to believe anyone can really love us and won't eventually leave us once they see how "bad" we are).

- Denial, isolation, control, shame, and inappropriate guilt are legacies from our family of origin. As a result of these symptoms, we feel hopeless and helpless.

- We have difficulty with intimacy, security, trust, and commitment in our relationships. Lacking clearly defined personal limits and boundaries, we become enmeshed in our partner's needs and emotions (i.e., become codependent).

- We tend to procrastinate and have difficulty following projects through from beginning to end.

- We have a strong need to be in control. We overreact to change things over which we have no control.[44]

---

44. Anonymous. Adult Children of Alcoholics, "List 2," accessed August 13, 2014.

Out of suffering have emerged the strongest souls.
The most massive characters are seared with scars.

—KHALIL GIBRAN
FROM *THE BROKEN WINGS*, 1912; IN ARABIC

CHAPTER 9

MY ROAD TO HEALING

As I previously mentioned, I did a lot of work with my therapist addressing the ramifications of my codependent relationship with my ex-husband; discovering I had been sexually abused at age two and then beginning the process of putting the pieces back together of a childhood riddled with parental narcissistic abuse.

For the duration of the time I was working with my therapist, I was also employed at an emotionally abusive non-profit agency providing therapy. In many ways, my experience at this job replicated the abuse I experienced as a child; but this time, I was an adult in a workplace environment. I was there for seven years and five months. Since it's difficult to describe what it was like there, perhaps my physical, emotional, and mental symptoms may give you some clues. I suffered from chronic insomnia (I nearly avoided getting into several accidents due to falling asleep at the wheel), and I developed high blood pressure (my blood pressure was actually low prior to this job). I had a short fuse (very unlike me). I was anxious, highly guarded to the point of being numb. I felt depressed (toward the end I told myself I preferred death to working at this place), and my self-esteem eventually reached an all-time low.

I was terrified of the people in charge, and they used fear to control their employees. It was as if for eight hours a day, I was a minion in a dictatorship. They really seemed to believe they were beyond the law and could do anything they wanted to us. The threat of being fired or written up always loomed. The management was adept at isolating you and making you feel like the worst employee ever, so you came to believe that no one else would want to hire you (hence you'd better stay where you are). Employees were not allowed to talk back or have any kind of voice. If you did, you were singled out, humiliated in front of everyone and then forced back into your place.

The five common features of brainwashing were present here: isolation, unpredictable attacks, accusations, humiliation, and threats. What differentiates narcissism in the workplace is the way the group dynamic is used to perpetuate the abuse. There came a point, however, when I had had enough, and I started saying exactly what I felt (even though I was well aware that the management would punish me). I never went so far as being disrespectful though. Truth be told, I really couldn't help myself anymore. As a result, I would just let loose and say what I thought.

In the past, when they were abusive, I found myself crippled in my ability to fight back because my ex-employers were masters of manipulation and adept at twisting my words. When I reached the point where I had had enough, I believe I was somehow able to reconnect with my lost rage, and this reconnection seemed to empower me to think critically once again (for the first time since childhood). I was no longer afraid of being fired because I honestly didn't care anymore. At the same time, I discovered from coworkers that it was highly unlikely that I would be fired because the management didn't want to pay unemployment. With no other job on the horizon, I found myself trapped like an abused, chained dog. By the time I decided to resign my position, however, I was able to stand, defend myself, and even gain some understanding of the manipulative and abusive tactics the management was using on me. Thus, you could say part of my healing involved remaining in the crucible of adversity until nearly all the bonds of the past were burned away. As a result, for the first time in my life, my long-term brain fog began to lift.

Another part of my healing was learning to forgive and let go. Research has shown that forgiveness can improve both mental and physical health.[45] I had to let go of all the trauma I had experienced in my life. I listened to Katie Souza as she taught about the demoniac in the Bible who dwelt among the tombs. Basically, she explained that the tombs represented traumas that I was going back to, remembering and replaying things that happened to me. The problem was that dwelling among the tombs gave the spirit of Legion (a thousand or more demons) the legal right to torment me in my mind, body, and soul. It appeared that this spirit in particular was the tormentor of the traumatized. [46] To be honest, I didn't really believe that it was possible to overcome all the trauma in my life simply by forgiving and applying the blood and resurrection power of Jesus Christ, to wash away all my soul-wounds and rid me of tombstones. But as I did so, I experienced more freedom, and the condemning voices in my head began to quiet down. I also seemed to be making more progress regarding my twenty-year struggle with insomnia.

Dwelling among the tombs wasn't the only issue. I was also traumatized by the countless storms of life that would metaphorically beat my boat over and over, threatening to sink me. Ironically, this was how I described my childhood to my therapist: I was out at sea and wave upon wave would crash over me, threatening to drown me. I felt all alone in the great expanse of the ocean, and I believed God was responsible for causing the waves to beat upon me even though I knew better. I felt I was taking in so much water that it was hard for me to come up for air. It was crucial for me to learn that the waves were "demonically inspired" rather than "divinely inspired," and that the purpose of the waves was to either get me to give up on ever reaching my destiny or to be severely traumatized by the storms themselves. I was disempowered even if I did manage to make it to my destination. Realizing that God hadn't initiated the storms prompted me to rethink my precarious/antagonistic relationship with him.

45. Weir, Kirsten. "Forgiveness Can Improve Mental and Physical Health," American Psychological Association, accessed December 31, 2018, www.apa.org/monitor/2017/01/ce-corner.aspx, page 2.

46. Souza, Katie. *Legion Slayer* (Eleven Eleven Enterprise, 2018). Audio.

Despite everything I knew about God from the Bible, I still projected sadistic attributes onto him because of my father. Understanding that the waves were demonically inspired also gave me a better understanding of what the actual purpose of the waves were. Until Katie Souza, I thought the waves were obstacles that I had to overcome in life, and I had a long history of giving up in defeat (but only after getting exhausted, discouraged, and frustrated) because they never seemed to end. I was finally able to correct my distorted perception of what was going on. I also took things a step further by realizing that God was positioned beside me, walking with me through the waves.

For me, learning to deal with the storms, although helpful in correcting my faulty perceptions, wasn't enough to get me any closer to my destiny. For most of my Christian life, there was an overarching theme of never reaching the promised shores. I struggled for over 30 years to get to the next level, to get some sort of breakthrough so I could edge closer to the destiny I felt God had for me. Without fail, I would encounter setbacks and blockages. There was an unmistakable pattern that kept reoccurring. I felt like I was cursed and beaten down into lowering my expectations. Other people would experience breakthroughs but mine were minimal for the most part. Robert Henderson spoke about having struggles similar to mine until he finally dealt with his own generational curses. God showed him in a dream, that because of something a deceased relative did, he was not legally able to release all that he had for Robert. If you take a closer look at the Bible, there are many instances where God was bound and unable to do what he wanted to do. Past events had created legal dilemmas which needed to be taken care of first. After repeating Robert's prayer to break generational curses, I had the greatest breakthrough in my whole life. Yes, I've said prayers to break generational curses before, but I never dealt with them in the courts of heaven with God as judge. I could literally feel a shift in the spiritual realm after the prayer, and my breakthrough came a few days later. Robert also mentioned a second key to experiencing more breakthroughs. He spoke about approaching God as judge and making a case regarding how we need God to move for his purposes to be fulfilled in our lives, rather than approaching God on the basis of need. Again, there are many examples of this in the Bible. According to Robert, this is an essential shift, as we need to pray apostolically for God's purposes to be fulfilled on the earth, rather than praying pastorally for our needs to be met.[47]

Making sense of my suffering has been a journey in itself. As a young child, I thought God was a sadist because he designed me to have emotions, yet he placed me in a family that seemed to thrive on destroying my emotions and causing me extreme pain any chance they got.

The fact that it didn't just happen once, but systematically throughout my childhood, further alienated me from God and made it much more difficult for me to forgive my parents. God continues to work with me on this, and Katie's teachings also have helped a lot in this area. I found the writings of Miroslav Volf helpful as well, as he was able to voice his own personal struggle with the issue of forgiveness when his country was wracked with civil war. He wrote:

> At the heart of the cross is Christ's stance of not letting the other remain an enemy and of creating space in himself for the offender to come in. Read as the culmination of the larger narrative of God's dealing with humanity, the cross says that despite its manifest enmity toward God humanity belongs to God; God will not be God without humanity. The cross is the giving up of God's self in order not to give up on humanity; it is the consequence of God's desire to break the power of human enmity without violence and receive human beings into divine communion... Forgiveness is therefore not the culmination of Christ's relation to the offending other; it is a passage leading to embrace. The arms of the crucified are open—a sign of space in God's self and an invitation for the enemy to come in.[48]

47. Henderson, Robert. "Breaking curses' legal rights." Youtube. July 2017. "Present yourcase," by Robert Henderson. Youtube. Internet. Books available at roberthenderson.org.

48. Volf, Miroslav. *Exclusion & Embrace: A Theological Exploration of Identity, Otherness, and Reconciliation* (TN: Abingdon Press, 1996) 126–127.

But where was God when I was being abused? He reminded me of a scene in the movie *Speed*. Sandra Bullock was handcuffed to a metal post of an out-of-control, speeding train that was about to fly off the remaining tracks. Keanu Reeves's efforts to get her freed were fruitless. She encouraged him to save himself while he could and jump off the train. Instead, she was visibly shaken as he chose to stay with her and proceeded to wrap his body around her as they prepared for impact.[49] God showed me through this clip that he endured everything I went through first. It helped to know that he knew exactly how I felt because he chose to experience it all on the cross for me.

I recently read about the actress Viola Davis's horrific childhood. It made me wonder what role her childhood experiences had in her becoming who she is now. She reported growing up in extreme poverty. The stench of urine was constant due to poor plumbing in her building. Her father was a violent drunk. She remembered having things thrown at her and going to sleep with the sound of rats chewing on her toys. As I used to work in tandem with the Department of Children and Family Services, I would say that had she come to the attention of the system, she would have been a prime candidate for removal from her home.[50] I have to ask (having seen it happen so many times) whether removal is an imposition of cultural values, that when exerted on an already difficult situation, is actually more horrifically detrimental than helpful.

I believe it is rarely ever a positive thing to remove a child from everything they have ever known. Removed children fondly report remembering things like the smell of their home or room. Someone once told me that families struggling with poverty are already barely holding it together and having a DCFS case open is the equivalent of the straw that breaks the camel's back. The family collapses and rarely, if ever, recovers. Yes, Viola would have likely been placed in a more comfortable home. What

49. *Speed*, Directed by Jan de Bont. Performances by Keanu Reeves and Sandra Bullock (Mark Gordon Productions, 1994).
50. Lang, Brent, "Viola Davis Knows What's Wrong with Hollywood…and How to Fix It," *Variety Magazine* (July 2018), page 1.

I question is whether doing so would have resulted in her becoming a world-class actress. Are we not, on some level, the sum total of our experiences? Consider the fact that if you open the eggshell of a hatching chick instead of allowing it to peck through independently, it will die.

Is it not within the struggle that we find ourselves, or better yet, find God? I used to ask the question why so many bad things have happened to me, but all I found were dead ends and no answers that proved satisfactory. My favorite theology professor used to say that there was no point in asking why bad things happen to people. Rather, the question we should concern ourselves with is, "What did you do with it?"

When I think about my own childhood and what would have happened had DCFS gotten involved with me and my family, I am confident I would not have ended up where I have. What the mental health system has done (which I find can be both helpful and hurtful) is promote the "victim mentality." It is easier to lean back on this as an excuse instead of working twice as hard to overcome it. It is like a crutch with splinters on it. If you don't eventually get off of it, you will get an armpit full of pain. Nevertheless, I did find the diagnostic side of it helpful in that it helped me to understand what was going on, especially regarding my relationship with my ex-husband.

When I was in graduate school studying the over five hundred theories of what was psychologically wrong with humanity, each theory seemed to have a grain of truth, but ultimately did not have a leg to stand on. I became discouraged and frustrated from having to study so many theories that ultimately failed to produce any substantial answers. That is until I learned about the Christian worldview. It is the macrolens through which I view the world and draw my beliefs about healing and redemption: 1) the real problem with the world and with my life is sin; 2) the solution and cure is Jesus Christ; 3) no matter what I've been through trauma wise, all of it is redeemable through him; and 4) not only can he heal me completely (something the mental health system admittedly fails to do), he can make me even better than I ever was before.

Redemptively speaking, since I have a history of being abused by a narcissist and being married to one, I have an insider understanding of the dynamics involved in domestic violence. God has turned things around by using my tragic experiences to help free many women from their past abuse. I believe that one day, when my non-profit goes international, and I am finally able to help children involved in prostitution and slavery, my life will have come full circle as I will symbolically be rescuing myself.

In the television program, *A Walk to Beautiful*, young girls became excluded from their community through no fault of their own. While growing up, they were given the responsibility of carrying heavy burdens on their backs for years and doing so had caused many of them to become barren. One girl who was so rejected and having had nowhere to go, ended up working in a home for orphaned children.[51] It was a wonderful and beautiful situation because each one needed the other. I believe this is how God works. Nothing we suffer is wasted. Every scar we bear is a beautiful testimony to the healing power of our God, who himself was wounded so he could embrace us.

51. *A Walk to Beautiful*, Directed by Mary Olive Smith and Amy Bucher, Engel Entertainment Production in association with NOVA. PBS, September 20, 2011.

Look what he's done to you. It isn't fair.
Your light was bright and new.
But he didn't care.
He took the heart of a little girl.
And made it grow up too fast.
Now words like innocence don't mean a thing.
You hear the music play. But you can't sing.
Those pictures in your mind
keep you locked up in your past.
This is a song for the broken girl.
The one pushed aside by the cold, cold, world.
You are. Here me when I say.
You're not the worthless they made you feel.
There is a love they can never steal away.
And you don't have to stay the broken girl.
Those damaged goods you see in your reflection.
Love sees them differently.
Love sees perfection.
A beautiful display.
Of healing on the way tonight.
Tonight.

LYRICS FOR "BROKEN GIRL" BY MATTHEW WEST,
FROM HIS ALBUM, *THE STORY OF YOUR LIFE*
(SPARROW RECORDS, 2010)

CHAPTER 10

HEADING IN THE RIGHT DIRECTION

The following is a quoted and combined list of signs that you've been raised by a narcissist:

- You have no sense of yourself, your wants, your needs, or your goals.

- You're a complete doormat.

- At times, you've felt you were more your parent's partner than their child.

- You are hyper-attuned to other people's emotional needs at the expense of your own.

- You are more likely to choose partners who are self-absorbed or emotionally volatile.

- You're afraid you might be a narcissist yourself.

- You are more vulnerable to anxiety, depression, and having a personality disorder yourself.

- You derive self-worth solely from your achievements.[52, 53]

---

52. Almendrala, Anna, "6 Signs You Were Raised by a Narcissist," accessed March 10, 2016, huffingtonpost.com/entry/6-ways-to-know-you-were-raised-by-narcissists_us_5616b091e4b008 2030a18f72, pages 1–8.

53. Hutchison, Christine, "The Impact of Growing Up with a Narcissistic or Borderline Parent," Psyched in San Francisco: A Center for Modern Psychotherapy, accessed October 3, 2016, psychedinsanfrancisco.com/impact-growing-narcissistic-borderline-parent/, pages 2–3.

Now that you have a better understanding of brainwashing, here are some steps I have taken in order to regain control of my mind and my life, which may prove helpful to you as well:

I am a Christian and it was really God who lead me to put many of the pieces of my life back together. He is my maker, after all, and has the original plans. Seeking him out will only benefit and accelerate your healing.

Find a therapist who is knowledgeable regarding narcissism and narcissistic abuse of children. Admittedly, there aren't many therapists who are knowledgeable in this specific area. If this is your experience, I suggest you seek out a Christian therapist who follows the lead of the Holy Spirit—as he will guide you into all truth.

Find other adult children of narcissists. It was an incredible relief for me when I discovered the blogspot for adult children of narcissists called *House of Mirrors* (you may also refer to my Resource Guide for this information). I realized for the first time that I wasn't alone and that there were other people like me who understood what I had been through. Most importantly, believed that my sufferings were real. The House of Mirrors blogspot is more akin to an archive of articles now, but the number of sites where you can connect to other adult children of narcissists has multiplied. Find a site where you feel comfortable and relish the company of others who can relate to you like very few people can.

Give yourself time to grieve. Being a child of a narcissist is in many ways like being an orphan because your parents were so completely consumed with themselves. Grieve for the parents you never had. Grieve for the childhood you never had. Cut yourself some slack too. You were immersed in a toxic environment. Hopefully, you now have the opportunity of being on the outside looking in. The worst is over.

I believe it is of utmost importance that you take the time to get to know who you are. Yes, it will be awkward at times and often painful. Due to the lack of nurturance and the fact that you were overshadowed by a narcissistic parent, never allowed to develop, makes this extremely important. Remember you are not a bother or an imposition to others, nor are your needs something to be ignored.

When I began therapy, there were big gaps of silence in my sessions mainly because I didn't know myself at all. Had my therapist filled up the silence with conversation, I wouldn't have been able to delve into the struggle to find myself. The fact that I have even written this book is evidence of the benefits of the struggle—I learned to write by documenting my feelings on a daily basis. Until you get to know who you are, it's best to give yourself some time to heal by remaining single. At this juncture, you resemble half a person trying to find another half to make a whole. It's called *codependence*, and it's a setup for disaster. Being a child of a narcissist makes you narcissistic "bait." You have been brainwashed and programed this way. You have a proclivity for being attracted to narcissists because they will happily fill the void within you that should have been filled by you. Remember exclusivity and control may look like love to someone who has been manipulated and controlled in the past, but they are *not* love.

Practice saying no and mean it. Easier said than done. While learning who you are, you also learn that you have value, and you have your own needs. In other words, "backing up your no" means valuing yourself enough to have a backbone. It does take practice because doing so will likely feel foreign, frighteningly awkward and too reminiscent of your narcissistic parent.

Nevertheless, it is healthy and it counters the factors that worked to make you a doormat in the first place. An added benefit is that as you get better at it, you will become less attractive to predators and abusers.

Learn to pay attention to your gut instincts. You were taught not to trust your own perceptions/gut instincts. You must begin to get your warning system working again. Practice paying attention to the red flags: fluttering in the stomach area, hair raised and inner warning voice. This system is instinctual. This will enable you to be better equipped to pick up on people and situations that are not healthy for you.

Curb your empathy. Children of narcissists seem to have an endless supply, and this is what abusive people look for. They want a partner who is going to give and give, and put up with a lot of abuse—far more than the average person would tolerate. If your friends comment on how your partner mistreats you, perk up your ears instead of brushing it off. Examine your family, friends, co-workers and romantic relationships. Take a hard look to see whether the relationships are reciprocal or one-sided (with you putting in the majority of the effort). If it's one-sided with you being the invested one, it's time to pull out.

Take care of yourself by putting your needs first, or at least second. This is probably the hardest thing to do because meeting other people's needs first is so ingrained in us. Doing so may seem narcissistic on the surface but it's not. Your value is *not* determined by all the things you do for others. Consider this more like self-care, burnout prevention, or better yet, de-programming. Remember, your needs are not a bother or an imposition.

You are not responsible for the feelings or happiness of anyone but yourself. The narcissist in your life trained you to believe you had no boundaries so they could have complete access to you. Boundaries go both ways—you need to have them, and you need to respect others' boundaries. Being a child of a narcissist means that you have a propensity to control others, and even if your means of control may be cloaked in kindness, call it what it is. The only person you can truly control is yourself. Otherwise, you will likely become an enabler, a codependent, a people pleaser, or possibly all three.

Find your voice and find your rage. As an adult, I had locked down my emotions so much that I could not scream, literally. I just didn't have it in me. Attending a church that was so loud that I couldn't hear the person singing next to me allowed me to effectively practice singing really loud and thus reconnect to my child-self. Examine your interests and carefully consider the things that interested you as a child. Find creative ways to release the emotions you have pent up inside you. It took a long time for me to find my rage. Metaphorically speaking, I think my journey has been from being a partially-assembled person to becoming more of a whole. Growing a backbone was an integral part of the process. Reconnecting with my anger was crucial to regaining my ability to think critically. Anger isn't all bad. It can be channeled so you can be empowered to do some amazing things.

You don't need to be in fight-or-flight mode anymore, but your body might be reacting otherwise. Although I am not a medical doctor, I strongly suggest that you consider the following information. Just as you wouldn't expect a recently released POW or a soldier returning home from war to suddenly acclimate to life in society, you are in many ways suffering as they were. Research has shown that being in fight-or-flight mode depletes your body of vital nutrients and especially puts a lot of strain on your adrenal system while increasing your cortisol levels. Adrenal fatigue is a stress-related condition not yet fully accepted by the medical community, but evidence for its viability continues to grow especially among women.[54] Surprisingly, recent research has shown that even though you may be out of the dangerous situation that caused you stress, severe illnesses can assail you years later.[55] Many of my domestic violence victims complained about not feeling like themselves even after leaving their abusive partners.

Marcelle Pick, MSN, OB-GYN, NP, described the three stages of adrenal fatigue mentioned below. Although each stage has distinct symptoms, there may be some overlap, as you may be transitioning, or on your way to total dysfunction or burn out. This adrenal fatigue list of symptoms will help you identify where you are on the adrenal fatigue spectrum. This is crucial for determining the best steps for supporting and bringing your adrenals back into balance for optimal functioning. Please refer to the website mentioned under footnote 57, or the "Health-Related Resources" section for more information.

---

54. Pick, Marcell, "What Causes Adrenal Fatigue? The Effects of High Cortisol Levels and What You Can Do About It," accessed December 6, 2018, www.marcellepick.com/adrenal-fatigue-effects-high-cortisol-levels-can/, pages 2–4.
55. "Beyond the Bruises Campaign: Domestic Violence and Chronic Illness," Women's Health Research Institute, Northwestern University, accessed December 6, 2018, www.womenshealth.northwestern.edu/blog/beyond-bruises-campaign-domestic-violence-Chronic-illness, page 1.

Wired (Phase 1)—Recognition of these symptoms can help prevent you from reaching the final stage of utter exhaustion.

- consuming a high quantity of calories in the evening
- weight gain in the abdominal region
- feeling like you are racing all day long
- high anxiety or panic attacks
- feelings of anger, depression, or frustration
- difficulty getting to sleep or staying asleep
- focus and concentration difficulty
- PMS or problems with menstrual periods, perimenopause or menopause
- low libido
- thyroid trouble

Wired and Tired (Phase 2)—As women move into this second phase, many of the same symptoms from the Wired list are present. What's confusing is that you'll also see symptoms that nearly contradict your original symptoms. This occurs as your adrenal glands can no longer keep up and are producing an insufficient amount of stress hormones. In this phase, you can expect to see:

- dependence on caffeine to keep you going
- trouble waking up in the morning
- daytime exhaustion
- low libido
- weight gain
- waking up with extreme anxiety

- digestive problems

- thyroid issues

- frustration, anger, or depression

- insomnia

- thinning hair

- weakened immune system

- dizziness or low blood pressure

- salt cravings

Tired (Phase 3)—If you ignore or fail to recognize all that comes before, you may find yourself in the final stage of adrenal imbalance. Although we call it the Tired phase, it likely doesn't even begin to describe the level of exhaustion you are feeling. These symptoms include:

- an absolute lack of energy

- unexplained weight gain that you can't get rid of, no matter what you try

- reliance on caffeine to function

- insulin resistance

- extreme cravings for salty or sugary foods, or refined carbohydrates

- feeling tired even after a full night's sleep

- low libido

- becoming overwhelmed at fairly minor challenge, responding poorly to stress[56]

---

56. Pick, *Adrenal Fatigue*, pages 5–8.

Do not fall in love because you believe you can help someone. I did this with my ex-husband, and it was a huge mistake. It's an issue our marriage counselor brought up. It's not fair to do this because you are not embracing the person you are with for who they are right now. Instead, you are falling in love with the potential in someone. This isn't fair to either one of you. For his part, he needs to help himself instead of relying on you. You are not responsible for him; you are only responsible for yourself.

Find a good Thai masseuse. As absurd as this sounds, I have reaped tons of benefits by getting massages on a weekly basis. I was a mess in the beginning in large part because my chronic insomnia had left my body very stiff and inflexible. Thai massage is unlike other types of massage because it is one of the oldest. You are massaged in more than one position, and you experience more health benefits than other massage types.[57]

The reason I suggest this is that our bodies hold the memories of trauma even if we are unable to speak about it. Through the process of massage, I was able to touch on some of the deep weariness I felt from having to constantly address others' needs since I was a small child. My masseuse also managed to discover a painful spot on my back where I believe I hold most of my pain.

For those of you who are overcoming abuse perpetrated by a narcissist on the more severe end of the spectrum, although it is difficult to wrap your head around this, you need to come to terms with this sobering fact—this type of narcissist tends to be a mental and emotional cannibal. His/her joy is some form of sadism. Your pain is his/her painkiller.[58] You are not the cause of your victimization as they often claim. Please be cautious and tentative if you happen to be dealing with this type of narcissist. Keep what was mentioned above in mind as you determine how much contact you are willing to give them.

---

57. Eske, Jamie, "What Are the Health Benefits of Thai Massage?" accessed December 20, 2018, www.medicalnewstoday.com/articles/323687.php, pages 2–4.

58. Lisette, "Malignant Narcissists Feed Off Your Pain," accessed February 16, 2016, house-of-mirrors.blogspot.com/2013/03/malignant-narcissists-feed-off-your-pain.html, pages 2 and 4.

Highly sensitive people (many of whom I believe are children of narcissists) tend to naturally attract abusive, predatorial, narcissistic types, but don't understand the reasons why. Quoted below are some of the reasons. Bear in mind some issues have been repeated, but they're worth mentioning once again.

- Our giving nature means we often put other people's needs before our own.

- We're so open that we take on other people's stuff like emotional storage containers.

- If you have low self-esteem, you can overlook the signs that things aren't right, that you aren't being treated right, so you ignore the injuries to yourself and let it continue.

- If you feel like a victim or have been victimized in the past, you will project that belief outward. Narcissists will pick up on it and hone in on you as a target.

- Adult children of narcissists sensitivity to other people's feelings means it can feel wrong to say no. We think since we can feel it, we must do something about it. But we are not responsible for other people's feelings.[59]

Since children of narcissists likely have no idea what a healthy relationship entails, here is a list of basic needs in healthy relationships quoted from Hein.

- the need for goodwill from others

- the need for emotional support

- the need to be heard by the other and to be responded to with respect and acceptance

---

59. Ward, Deborah. "The Relationship between Sensitive People and Narcissists," accessed December 26, 2018, psychologytoday.com/us/blog/sense-and-sensitivity/201305/the-relationship-between-sensitive- people-and-narcissists.

- the need to have your own view, even if others have a different view

- the need to have your feelings and experience acknowledged as real

- the need to receive a sincere apology for any jokes or actions you find offensive

- the need for clear, honest, and informative answers to questions about what affects you

- the need for freedom from accusation, interrogation, and blame

- the need to live free from criticism and judgement

- the need to have your work and your interests respected

- the need for encouragement

- the need for freedom from emotional and physical threat

- the need for freedom from angry outbursts and rage

- the need for freedom from labels which devalue you

- the need to be respectfully asked rather than ordered

- the need to have your final decisions accepted

- the need for privacy at times[60]

60. Hein, Steve. "Emotional Abuse," accessed August 13, 2014, eqi/eabuse1.htm, pages 5–6.

RESOURCE GUIDE

- *Alias* (television series). I found watching the series therapeutic in that the storyline is about spies (no trust, constant deception, betrayal, and danger), and the family of the lead character is highly manipulative and shifty. Each show highlights the emotional turmoil that the lead character is going through. I was often able to show my therapist scenes from the show to illustrate my experience.

- Clayton, Ian. *Sonofthunder.org.* Ian relentlessly pursued God and he responded with incredible intimacy and revelation into the kingdom within us (as well as the kingdom of heaven). His teachings are literally "mindblowing" and healing as well.

- Drake, Dan. "DARVO: Understanding a Gaslighting Strategy of Reversing Blame," accessed January 20, 2020, banyantherapy.com. DARVO is an acronym (deny, attack, reverse, victim, offender) used to describe a pattern of emotional abuse often present in relationships, where one partner desires to intentionally distort the reality of the other. It's a means of gaining control of the victim through deception as she/he is unaware of the behavior the abuser is truly engaged in. I feel DARVO is an eye-opener in that it exposes and explains the confusing dance of betrayal that often leads to brainwashing.

- Hein, Steve. *Emotional Abuse.* equi.org/eabuse1.htm. This is an excellent site for gaining an understanding of emotional abuse.

- *House-of-mirrors.blogspot.com.* A blog about adult children of narcissist families and the fight to survive narcissistic abuse. The original site is now more of an archive of articles by adult children of narcissists, many if not all are very informative and eye-opening. This was one of the first resources I came across that encouraged me tremendously by showing me that I was not alone.

- Keesee, Gary. *Garykeesee.com*. If you want to do the impossible and enjoy the incredible, you need to understand how faith works. Gary Keesee's life is like the book of Acts because he understands how the kingdom of God operates.

- Louis de Canonville, Christine. *Narcissisticbehavior.net*. Christine is a therapist and expert in narcissism, especially from a personal and criminal point of view. She resides in Ireland, and has written many books on narcissism which may be purchased via her website.

- Miller, Alice. *The Drama of the Gifted Child; The Search for the True Self*. N. Y.: Basic Books, 1997. Print. Alice is a therapist who explores the origins and effects of childhood emotional abuse via client cases and works cited.

- Norwood, Robin. *Women Who Love Too Much*. Robin's book was on the New York Times bestseller list and remains in print. Her book addresses codependence, the factors leading up to it, and how to get out of it.

- Weir, Kirsten, "Forgiveness Can Improve Mental and Physical Health," American Psychological Association, accessed December 31, 2018, www.apa.org/monitor/2017/01/ce-corner.aspx. This article offers a blueprint for incorporating forgiveness in your life (that anyone can use regardless of your belief system).

HEALTH-RELATED RESOURCES

---

1. womentowomenhealthcarecenter.com
   Adrenal fatigue symptoms (both psychological and physical).
   Information on treatment.

2. diabeteslibrary.org/view.aspx?url=stress_b_vitamins
   Article discusses how stress can cause specific nutritional deficiencies
   and also lists some supplements to address them.

3. http://cdv.org/what-is-cdv/the-impact/
   If you are a child of a narcissist, chances are good that you were also
   exposed to domestic violence. This website provides information on child-
   hood domestic violence. The symptoms of which would likely be comorbid
   with the symptoms of narcissistic abuse and somewhat difficult to tease out.

BIBLIOGRAPHY

"What Is Narcissistic Personality Disorder? What Are the Symptoms of Narcissistic Personality Disorder?" accessed November 11, 2015, www.bandbacktogether.com/adult-children-of-Narcissistic-parents-resources/, pages 1–3, 5–6.

Krill Jr., William E., "The Child Victim of a Narcissistic Personality Disordered Parent," accessed October 25, 2017, https://wehavekids.com/family-relationships/the-child-victim-of-a-narcissistic-personality-Disordered-parent, page 1.

Declassified Documents 1984, Microfilms under MKULTRA (84) 002258, Central Intelligence Agency, Washington 25, DC, Office of the Director, April 1956, Research Publication (Woodbridge, CT: 1956), pages 3–8, 10.

Central Intelligence Agency, "Brainwashing from a Psychological Viewpoint," accessed November 21, 2018, www.cia.gov/library/readingroom/docs/CIA-RDP65-00756R000400050004-9.pdf 38, pages 18–25, 37–39.

Miller, Alice, *The Drama of the Gifted Child: The Search for the True Self* (NY: Basic Books, 1997) 30, 73, 87.

The Experiment, Directed by Paul T. Scheuring. Performances by Adrien Brody, and Forest Whitaker. Inferno; Magnet; Mercator; Adelstein Productions, 2010. Film.

McLeod, Saul, "The Stanford Prison Experiment," accessed December 19, 2018, https://simplypsychology.org/zimbardo.html, page 1.

"Brainwashing," accessed January 8, 2013, changingminds.org/techniques/conversion/brainwashing.htm, page 1.

Bonchay, Bree, "Narc-sadistic Brainwashing: The 8 Ingredients of Mind Control," accessed March 10, 2016, http://relationshipedia.me/2015/07/10/narc-sadistic-brainwashing-the-8-ingredients-of-mind-control/, pages 7–8.

Mega, Lesly Tamarin; Mega, Jessica Lee; Mega, Benjamin Tamarin; and Harris, Beverly Moore, *Brainwashing and Battering Fatigue, Psychological Abuse in Domestic Violence*, NCMJ, vol. 61, no. 6 (September/October 2000), pages 261–262.

"Goodbye, Farewell and Amen." *M*A*S*H.* Directed by Alan Alda, season 11, episode 16 (256 overall). Twentiethth Television, February 28, 1983. Television.

"Double Bind," accessed October 14, 2013, www.en.m.wikipedia.org., page 1.

Bateson, G., "Steps to an Ecology of the Mind: a Revolutionary Approach to Man's Understanding of Himself," *Double Bind, 1969* (Chicago: University of Chicago Press, 1972), pages 271–278.

Guillaume, Patricia, "The Double Bind: The Intimate Tie between Behavior and Communication," accessed April 23, 2008, www.abusesanctuary.blogspot.com, pages 3–4, 6.

Watzlawick, Paul; Beavin Bavelas, Janet; Jackson, Don D., *Pragmatics of Human Communication: A Study of Interactional Patterns, Pathologies, and Paradoxes* (New York, NY: W. W. Norton & Company Inc., 1967), pages 217–218.

Dahl, R., *Charlie and the Chocolate Factory* (NY.: A. A. Knopf, 1964) 23.

Monika, "Blinded, Bound, and Burdened: Parental Alienation and Two Theories—the Double Bind & Cognitive Dissonance," accessed October 14, 2013, www.parentalalienationsupport.com, page 3.

L. Nolan, Jeannette. "Learned Helplessness," accessed December 18, 2018, www.britannica.com/science/learned-helplessness, pages 1–2.

Billy Jack, Directed by Tom Laughlin. Performances by Tom Laughlin and Delores Taylor. National Student Film Corporation, 1971. Film.

"Reckoning," *Alias*, Directed by Daniel Attias, season 1, episode 6. Buena Vista Television, November 18, 2001. Television.

Prager, Dennis, "Brainwashing Children, Narcissistic Parents," accessed February 7, 2012, www.brainwashingchildren.com/2011/01/the-narcissistic-parent/, page 2.

Dauder, Alphonse. *Lettres de mon Moulin.*

Hein, Steve. "Emotional Abuse," accessed August 13, 2014, eqi/eabuse1.htm, pages 2–6. "Domestic Abuse May Affect Children in Womb," accessed December 6, 2018, www.sciencedaily.com/releases/2014/12/141216100628.htm, page 1.

Geringer Woititz, Janet. "List 1—Based on Studies of Adult Children of Alcoholics," accessed August 13, 2014, eqi.org/eabuse1/htm, 7–9.

Adult Children of Alcoholics, "List 2," accessed August 13, 2014.

Weir, Kirsten. "Forgiveness Can Improve Mental and Physical Health," American Psychological Association, accessed December 31, 2018, www.apa.org/monitor/2017/01/ce-corner.aspx, page 2.

Souza, Katie. *Legion Slayer,* (Eleven Eleven Enterprise, 2018). Audio.

Volf, Miroslav. *Exclusion & Embrace: A Theological Exploration of Identity, Otherness, and Reconciliation* (TN: Abingdon Press, 1996) 126–127.

Speed, Directed by Jan de Bont. Performances by Keanu Reeves and Sandra Bullock (Mark Gordon Productions, 1994). Film.

Lang, Brent, "Viola Davis Knows What's Wrong with Hollywood…and How to Fix It," *Variety Magazine* (July 2018), page 1.

A Walk to Beautiful, Directed by Mary Olive Smith and Amy Bucher, Engel Entertainment Production in association with NOVA. PBS, September 20, 2011. Television.

Almendrala, Anna, "6 Signs You Were Raised by a Narcissist," accessed March 10, 2016, huffingtonpost.com/entry/6-ways-to-know-you-were-raised-by-narcissists_us_5616b091e4b008 2030a18f72, pages 1–8.

Hutchison, Christine, "The Impact of Growing Up with a Narcissistic or Borderline Parent," Psyched in San Francisco: A Center for Modern Psychotherapy, accessed October 3, 2016, psychedinsanfrancisco.com/impact-growing-narcissistic-borderline-parent/, pages 2–3.

Pick, Marcell, "What Causes Adrenal Fatigue? The Effects of High Cortisol Levels and What You Can Do About It," accessed December 6, 2018, www.marcellepick.com/adrenal-fatigue-effects-high-cortisol-levels-can/, pages 2–4.

"Beyond the Bruises Campaign: Domestic Violence and Chronic Illness," Women's Health Research Institute, Northwestern University, accessed December 6, 2018, www.womenshealth.northwestern.edu/blog/beyond-bruises-campaign-domestic-violence- Chronic-illness, page 1.

Pick, Marcelle, "The Most Common Adrenal Fatigue Symptoms List," accessed December 26, 2018, www.marcellepick.com/common-symptoms-adrenal-fatigue/, pages 5–8.

Eske, Jamie, "What Are the Health Benefits of Thai Massage?" accessed December 20, 2018, www.medicalnewstoday.com/articles/323687.php pages 2–4.

Lisette, "Malignant Narcissists Feed Off Your Pain," accessed February 16, 2016, house-of-mirrors.blogspot.com/2013/03/malignant-narcissists-feed-off-your-pain.html, pages 2, 4.

Ward, Deborah. "The Relationship between Sensitive People and Narcissists," accessed December 26, 2018, psychologytoday.com/us/blog/sense-and-sensitivity/201305/the-relationship-between-sensitive- people-and-narcissists.

ABOUT THE AUTHOR

Sydney Kisai *(pen name)* is a Licensed Marriage and Family Therapist with extensive experience working with children, adolescents, couples, and families. She has also worked in collaboration with the Department of Children and Family Services, Probation, and the Domestic Violence and Family Preservation Programs. Always up for a challenge, she is especially adept at establishing a therapeutic alliance with clients, acknowledged by researchers as the most robust indicator of therapeutic success.

CPSIA information can be obtained
at www.ICGtesting.com
Printed in the USA
LVHW050718271021
701668LV00010B/508

9 781644 689721